SETTING BOUNDARIES TO FIND PEACE

WITH

NARCISSISTS & CODEPENDENTS

HOW TO COMMUNICATE WITH TOXIC PEOPLE TO FREE YOURSELF FROM MANIPULATION AND GASLIGHTING WITHOUT FEELING GUILTY

Robert J. Charles, PhD, DMin

SETTING BOUNDARIES TO FIND PEACE WITH NARCISSISTS & CODEPENDENTS

How to Communicate with Toxic People to Free
Yourself From Manipulation and Gaslighting
Without Feeling Guilty

By Robert J. Charles, PhD, DMin

been derived from various sources. Please consult a licensed professional before attempting any techniques outlined in this book.

By reading this document, the reader agrees that under no circumstances is the author responsible for any losses, direct or indirect, which are incurred as a result of the use of the information contained within this document, including, but not limited to, errors, omissions, or inaccuracies.

Contents

Introduction 3

Part One: Explaining Codependency and Narcissism 8

Chapter One: The Overused Labels 10

How to Know If Someone Is a Narcissist or
Just Plain Abusive... 12

Understanding What NPD Is All About............................. 13

Traits of a Person with NPD 15

Types of Narcissists and What They Do.............................. 18

Codependent or Obsessive? 21

Traits of Dependent Personality Disorder 23

Signs You're in a Codependent Relationship 24

Chapter 1 Takeaway... 32

Chapter Two: Narcissism-Codependency Dynamics........ 34

The Dance Between the Narcissist and the Codependent 35

A Narcissist vs. a Codependent: Is One Better
Than the Other?... 37

Can a Person Be Both Codependent and a Narcissist? 39

Behavioral Patterns and Characteristics of Codependency ... 41

Why You Should Deal with Narcissistic-Codependent
Relationships Quickly 43

Chapter Two Takeaway 50

Chapter Three: Building Immunity Against the Weapons of
a Narcissist 51

Understand How a Narcissist Thinks 52

Handling Guilt Tripping.. 54

Handling Gaslighting.. 56

Handling Love Bombing 58

Handling Triangulation.. 60

Handling Playing the Victim 62

Handling Projections... 64

Handling Smear Campaigns 66

Chapter Three Takeaway... 71

Chapter Four: Detoxification From Toxic Relationships..72

Understanding the Six Relationship Types and Their Impact
on Your Life 73

Signs You're in a Toxic Relationship.................................. 78

Six Main Types of Toxic People 81

What Being in a Toxic Relationship Does to You 83

Chapter Four Takeaway.. 87

Chapter Five: Overcoming Narcissism and Codependency
in Origin Families 88

The Enmeshed Family System and How it Works.............. 89

Dealing with Narcissistic Siblings 91

Codependent Siblings.. 95

Chapter Five Takeaway.. 100

Chapter Six: Tips for Setting Healthy Boundaries..........101

Why You Need to Set Boundaries..................................... 102

Myths Holding You Back From Setting
Healthy Boundaries 104

How to Set Boundaries with Your Family......................... 106

Tactics for Setting Boundaries and
Maintaining Friendships... 108

How to Create Boundaries in the Workplace for a More
Positive Working Environment... 109

Setting Boundaries with Your Partner.............................. 111

How to Express Your Boundaries and Avoid Arguments... 114

How to Handle People Who Violate Your Boundaries...... 116

Chapter Six Takeaway.. 121

Part Two: Emotional Abuse Recovery............................122

Chapter Seven: What to Do When You Can't Leave:

Communicating with a Toxic Person............................. 123

Why Narcissists Are Hard to Reason With........................ 124

How to Communicate with a Toxic Person and Still Keep

Your Sanity 130

Expressing Your Needs and Truth in Every Relationship... 133

Figuring Out When You Should and Shouldn't be Sorry .. 136

Saying No Without Feeling Guilty.................................... 138

Chapter Seven Takeaway.. 143

Chapter Eight: Loving and Prioritizing Yourself When

Dealing with Narcissists 144

Overcoming Narcissistic Victim Syndrome for Good........ 145

Detoxifying After Years of Emotional Abuse..................... 147

Don't Blame Yourself.. 152

How to Prioritize Yourself Every Day............................... 153

Support Systems and Support Groups 155

Emotional Detoxification Worksheet 157

Radical Self-Love Worksheet.. 158

Self-Reflection and Self-Compassion for

Healing Worksheet.. 159

Chapter Eight Takeaway 160

A Much-Needed Biblical Roundup............................162

Conclusion 166

References 169

WANT TO OVERCOME OVERTHINKING and MANAGE DIFFICULT PEOPLE?

These **4 FREE** offers are perfect for you: 2 eBooks + 2 audiobooks

In these 2 eBooks + 2 audiobooks, YOU will discover:

- The three different forms of overthinking and how to spot them.
- How ruminating and worrying can damage your social life.
- The types of toxic people and how to escape their web of crises.
- How to discover if you are a highly sensitive person and ways to deal with that.

If you want to finally stop overthinking and being manipulated by others...

Scan this QR code to get these 4 FREE offers

1

SECOND BONUS

How to Face Any Challenge with Confidence

Download these **FREE 30 BIBLICAL PROMISES** to discover some powerful promises for **YOU**.

30 **BIBLICAL PROMISES** TO OVERCOME ANY CHALLENGE

At some point, everyone on this Earth faces a tough challenge. Help is on the way! God has your back. His Word will empower you to face any trial or tribulation. These 30 promises from God will give you the strength and resilience you need to move forward.

To get your **FREE** 30 BIBLICAL PROMISES TO OVERCOME ANY CHALLENGE, **click on this link:**

Scan this QR code to get these Promises.

Introduction

You are strong, You are firm, You are stable.

To start this book, I'd like to share this story with you.

I first heard about the concept of setting up boundaries a couple of days after my 23rd birthday. I was having issues with my friends, as they were intent on dictating every aspect of my life. I needed to keep them away from me but I didn't know how. Someone spoke to me about setting boundaries, and I was genuinely shocked that something like that existed.

You must understand why. I grew up with no notion of privacy and was taught that I was responsible for the happiness of my siblings. I was cast in this role and I had no choice but to act as though I liked it, even though I was often disrespected in the process. I lived with this discontentment all my life till I became an adult, and one day, I snapped. I wasn't going to take it anymore, and I let everyone know.

Somehow, I believed my declaration would be met with approval, with encouragement. (I know, I was painfully naive.) Eventually, *my enforcement of my boundaries led to being ostracized by my family and having my reputation massacred. But it paid off. Slowly, I started learning how to respect myself and ensure I behaved in a way that was kind to others, yet not disrespectful to myself. Boundaries won me my life back and gave me the foundation to create the kind of life I desired for myself.*

—*Sam*

So you're stuck with a toxic person in your life, or you've had an encounter (or maybe five) with a narcissist and you're tired of being cannon fodder for their manipulative behavior? Or maybe you're not really even sure if you're being manipulated. You've heard the words "narcissism" and "codependency" so often that you're more than a little confused about what they really mean. You may not even be sure about what a "toxic person" is or how to identify them. Well, reading this book is the best decision you could've made, and I'll show you why.

I find that the first step to effective learning and eventual transformation is to demystify misconceptions and shatter illusions. In the first part of this book, we'll be looking at what narcissism means. We'll examine the typical characteristics of the average narcissist and how you can identify one. You'll learn how to tell the difference between someone who's a narcissist and someone who's abusive (they're not necessarily mutually exclusive). We'll bust all the myths you may be harboring about narcissism, too.

Next, we'll look at what codependency is, how it's different from being narcissistic, and the connections between narcissism and codependency. What does psychology have to say about these two terms? How can you tell if you're in a codependent relationship? Is a narcissist better than a codependent person?

Then you'll find out if it's really possible to be free of manipulation and toxic gaslighting. We'll see how to prevent yourself from falling for the same narcissistic tactics over and over again. You'll learn how to respond to those behaviors in a way that leaves you with your dignity and self-respect intact.

Next up, have you ever tried taking a look at all your social connections to identify the toxic people in your life? I think this is necessary because for most of us, family and friends are a very big blind spot when it comes to identifying toxicity. How can you handle narcissistic family members? What's the best way to deal with codependent parents and siblings? We'll look at real-life examples and scenarios. You'll learn how to identify these traits in your family members, coworkers, and close friends. You'll learn how to mentally condition yourself to handle them and the best time to let go, if necessary.

Armed with the knowledge you've gained from the earlier parts of the book, we'll dive into the last section and seek to teach you the importance of setting boundaries and the most practical ways to do it. You'll learn how to create boundaries at work, with your family, and even with your significant other. You'll learn how to avoid unnecessary arguments and bickering by expressing your boundaries and reinforcing them. You'll see how to handle toxic people that you can't walk away from (without losing your mind) and how to say no without falling for the guilt trap.

Perhaps the most important thing you'll learn in this book is the need to love and prioritize yourself because that's anathema to a narcissist who's trying to manipulate someone. You'll discover how to stop blaming yourself and get rid of the effects of toxicity in your life. You'll get to use practical exercises and worksheets to apply the things you've learned and replicate your results with every relationship you have.

Many people can't stop talking about what they call "the Great Disparity." If you're wondering what that is, it's simply the fact that while a lot of emphasis is placed on people going to school to get educated, most of the truly important stuff you need to learn isn't taught in school—topics like emotional intelligence, setting boundaries, financial intelligence, and simple things like making relationships work. The most unfortunate aspect here is that most people don't even *know* what they don't know. They don't know what they need, and even if they do, they're not motivated enough to learn about it and diligently apply that knowledge, just like they would in school.

That's why I can boldly say that you deserve great praise for choosing to buy this book and learn this essential life skill. I'm not one to patronize people; the truth is, the fact that you're motivated enough to be here shows that you're programmed to be successful at this. It shows that you have the grit and tenacity to do what needs to be done. Even if you don't feel like it, there's a deep well of courage and strength available within you to guide you to where you need to be.

I'm not going to deceive you or sugarcoat the facts: there's a lot of work to be done. There's a lot of soul-searching and brutal honesty needed here. You'll have to be willing to dig deep into hurtful memories and come to terms with unpleasant truths about yourself. You'll have to abandon previously held conceptions about yourself and the people you love. You'll have to break yourself down and build your real self back up. You may cry in the process, or even feel tempted to set this book aside and give up at some point. But I'm more than confident that you can handle it. I also know that this book will be a turning point for you.

Finally, throughout the book, I have applied a biblical approach to addressing these issues, and at the end of each chapter, you'll find a quick workbook to help you integrate what you've learned.

Now, without spending any more time introducing the topic— let's delve right into it, shall we?

—Robert

PART ONE

Explaining Codependency and Narcissism

The great thing about the age of social media is the fact that information spreads faster than wildfire. This has a lot of advantages, primarily that people who need essential knowledge can get access to it with a snap of their fingers. Unfortunately, this comes with disadvantages too. I think the greatest drawback is the spread of incomplete and untrue information, which, as we all know, can have debilitating effects (Menczer & Hills, 2020).

The same holds true for the concepts of toxicity, narcissism, and codependency. You don't have to scroll too far on any social media before you come across someone teaching you stuff (which is untrue most of the time) and leading you to draw erroneous conclusions about yourself and other people.

Instead of playing at guessing or harboring any sort of uncertainty about this important issue, this first part will be about how to recognize narcissism and codependency. We'll examine if all abusive people are narcissistic and even how to tell if you're being abused by a narcissist. We'll look at the nitty-gritty of codependency and we'll check if other buzzwords, like "obsession," "dependency," and "trauma," are actually relevant in this scenario.

A fair number of people I've interacted with couldn't tell if they were codependent or even if they were in a codependent relationship. You may be in the same boat: you could be mistaking an unhealthy, codependent partnership for "true love" or a codependent friendship for a loyal one. We'll see the truth about that once and for all here.

Oh, and what about people that are both narcissistic and codependent? Is that really a thing and is that important to know? Yes, it's important to find out as much about the narcissistic person in your life as possible. You need to know why you should address the narcissistic codependent cycle in your life, even if it feels good some of the time.

By the end of this part, you'll be clear on the inner workings of narcissism and codependency. You'll stop throwing those buzzwords around carelessly and you'll be able to speak and act with confidence. We take a lot of time to break things down here so you'll have a clear understanding of what you're dealing with. I daresay that by the end of this part, you'll be able to predict the next move the narcissist or toxic person in your life will make, and you'll even have an idea of how to stop them in their tracks. This part is all about enlightenment, which is a vital step for empowerment.

The Overused Labels

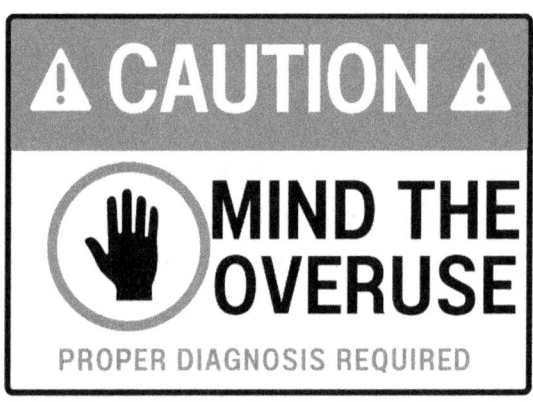

"Thorns and snares are in the way of the crooked;
whoever guards his soul will keep far from them."

—Proverbs 22:5 ESV

"When I look at narcissism through the vulnerability lens, I see
the shame-based fear of being ordinary. I see the fear of never
feeling extraordinary enough to be noticed, to be lovable, to
belong, or to cultivate a sense of purpose."

—Brené Brown

It was a sunny afternoon and I was out on the porch, having a glass of iced tea and trying to decide if I wanted to go for a walk because it was a particularly beautiful day. I remember this day because I had my sunglasses on and I looked at the sky through them. Of course, because of how opaque the glasses were, I didn't get to see the clear, pretty blue of the sky, nor the blindingly white fluffy clouds clearly.

It was at this point that I got a call from Sally, a young woman who was distressed because she claimed that her husband was a narcissist and an abuser. I quickly calmed her down and we scheduled a meeting. When we met, she told me that she'd been unhappy in her marriage and she just realized that her husband was a narcissist, thanks to a helpful TikTok video she saw. When we examined his behavior, her behavior, and what narcissism truly was, she had to reluctantly admit that she was wrong on a few counts.

I got together with Sally and her husband, and thankfully, they were able to clear up their issues because they were both invested in their marriage. I sat out on the porch after my last meeting with them and realized that Sally had been the victim of misinformation. She couldn't see her husband for who he really was, or his faults for what they were, because her vision was blocked by false perceptions, much like when I observed the sky through my sunglasses.

—Olivia

Are you in the same situation as Sally in the story above? Let's find out.

How to Know If Someone Is a Narcissist or Just Plain Abusive

Did you know that narcissism can and should be officially diagnosed by a mental health expert? (Cleveland Clinic, 2020). Have you ever heard of narcissistic personality disorder? Yes, it's a whole thing and there's a specific guideline for its diagnosis.

I'd like to ask you a question, if you don't mind. How many people have you labeled as a "narcissist" just because you didn't like a particular behavior or attitude? Did you know that even the average, "normal" person is manipulative to an extent? Did you know that even innocent children can be manipulative too? So, where do you draw the line? How can you clearly detect an abusive person or tell if they're narcissistic or even codependent?

The fact is that while we admit that abuse can occur in various ways and affect various aspects of one's life, not every abusive person is a narcissist. Don't get me wrong, being abused is detrimental, no matter what form it takes—but it's important for us to be specific about the personality of the abuser and the type of abuse. This is because each abusive personality has different effects on their victim and a thorough knowledge is needed for healing to be effective.

Another interesting tidbit is that, according to clinical therapist Dr. Alyssa Mancao (2020), people with narcissistic behaviors do not automatically have narcissistic personality disorder. This means that even though the people in our lives may exhibit some narcissistic behaviors, we can't just diagnose them with a disorder.

Narcissistic abuse is centered on the abuser and is a reflection of the fact that they lack empathy, have an inflated sense of self-importance, and need to be admired. All their narcissistic behaviors stem from these major roots, and any abuse that's perpetrated for reasons outside these can't be qualified as narcissistic abuse.

Understanding What NPD Is All About

Narcissistic Personality Disorder (NPD) is a mental health disorder characterized by a need for special treatment or admiration, a sense of self-importance or grandiosity, and a consistent fantasy of exaggerated power (Kacel et al., 2017). According to the 5th edition of the Diagnostic and Statistical Manual of Mental Disorders (DSM-5), NPD is classified as a "Cluster B" personality disorder. This class of disorders involves dramatic, emotional, and erratic behavior. NPD one of the personality disorders that is diagnosed least often (Pies, 2011).

A lack of empathy in addition to a need for special attention and feelings of grandiosity are hallmarks of NPD (Ronningstam & Weinberg, 2013). It is interesting to note that people with NPD often have an air of confidence or arrogance and may be described as condescending. However, in actuality, these individuals usually struggle with low self-esteem and feelings of inadequacy.

I've already mentioned that a lot of people may exhibit narcissist traits, but there's a particular set of criteria that has to be met before NPD is diagnosed. Of course, people that have NPD are greatly affected when it comes to their interpersonal relationships and their life in general. More often than not, they try to control and manipulate those around them even when it's harmful to others.

According to the American Psychiatric Association, NPD usually starts when the narcissist is in early adulthood (APA, 2013), and it is more common in men than women (Ronningstam & Weinberg, 2013). So when can we definitively say that someone has NPD?

Well, Dr. Zach Rosenthal (as cited by Biggers, 2022) believes that NPD can be diagnosed when someone exhibits any five of these nine characteristics:

1. A desire and a tendency to oppress others

2. A lack of empathy

3. An exaggerated sense of self-importance

4. An obsession with fantasies of fame and brilliance

5. A resentment of others or a belief that other people are resentful of them

6. A thirst for undue attention and admiration

7. A belief that they are extraordinary or special and can only be understood by other special people and they should only associate with other special people

8. A sense of entitlement

9. A tendency to exhibit conceited or egotistical behaviors

Of course, this diagnosis is best made by a mental health expert, but I believe it's easy to put two and two together by yourself, especially if you've taken the pains to do the proper research. If you have a narcissist in your life, you may believe that it's easier for you to just go with the flow and put up with their excessive behaviors, especially because they don't know how to handle criticism or disagreement.

Unfortunately, you'll find that doing this will only stretch you till you break. And the narcissist will still demand that you stretch further. Isn't it better to find out how to handle them once and for all without losing (any more of) yourself?

Traits of a Person with NPD

According to the American Psychological Association's dictionary, a trait is "*an enduring personality characteristic that describes or determines an individual's behavior across a wide range of situations"* (APA, n.d.).

Furthermore, Encyclopedia Britannica defines personality as "a characteristic way of thinking, feeling, and behaving." That means a person's personality is their habitual or default way of being in the world. It affects their attitude, mood, and even their opinions, and it's how we each make our mark on the world (Holzman, 2023). If we follow this line of thought, a trait is also a person's habitual behaviors, thought patterns, and feelings. People with a particular trait are naturally inclined to behave in that particular way the vast majority of the time, all things being equal.

It's extremely important to highlight these differences here so that you have a clear understanding of the condition and you'll be able to assess someone's behavior and thought patterns before you slap the narcissist label on them. Let's take a deeper look at the habitual behaviors, thoughts, and feelings (the traits) of someone with NPD:

Lack of empathy

Narcissists often do not have the capacity, or have a limited capacity, to understand or care about anyone else's feelings. They have a hard time apologizing and can't view matters from another person's perspective. A narcissistic partner or friend can't truly validate your feelings or understand you because of this trait.

Frequent attempts to monopolize conversations and gatherings

Talking over others, interrupting them, and directing the conversation back to themselves or to their achievements is a common narcissistic trait that may be easy to spot. The typical narcissist believes that they deserve to be in the spotlight no matter where they are and will stop at nothing to achieve that. This feeds into their need for special attention and their desire to be recognized and also pacifies their internal struggle with low self-esteem.

Overblown sense of self-importance

The average narcissist is convinced that they're the best thing since sliced bread—and they don't keep that to themselves. They feel that they are special, superior, or set apart from everyone else and that they deserve to only mingle with other special people like them. To top it all off, they also have grand fantasies about gaining massive power, admiration, fame, or even love.

Shallow relationships

Most narcissists are not capable of showing empathy, and this is reflected in the quality of relationships they have with others. No matter how intense or committed they may seem to someone, they view relationships as transactional and they only participate when they have a lot to gain.

They never want to take the blame, are convinced that other people are jealous of them, are jealous of everyone, and they have no qualms about pretending to love you just to get you attached to them. They love to have control over their relationships and will do anything to retain said control, no matter how dramatic. They are also very vengeful and do not like being criticized, corrected, or disagreed with.

Gaslighting

This is another popular buzzword that refers to the situation when someone says or does something to you and later denies the words or actions in such an expert manner that you're convinced you hallucinated those events. They do this to make you discredit your own senses and rely on their judgment rather than your own.

There are a lot of narcissistic traits apart from these popular ones which come up in different forms in response to certain social behaviors. A narcissist's traits also depend on what kind of narcissist they are.

Types of Narcissists and What They Do

Something a lot of people struggle with is acknowledging that their partner, parent, or any other loved one is a narcissist, especially after they've done a lot of research on NPD. Even though they may identify one or two traits, they simply refuse to believe that someone they love lacks empathy or is manipulative. This is mostly because narcissists are great at pretending. They will pretend to be friendly, warm, loving, or generous—whatever it takes to keep you on their hook!

There are various types of narcissists, and you may recognize someone you know in one of these subtypes:

1. The overt or obvious narcissist

This is also known as grandiose narcissism or agentic narcissism. They fit the typical description of a narc: they are arrogant, confident, assertive, competitive, aggressive, and they always strive to be the center of attention. They are most likely selfish, overbearing, and stubborn. They have an exaggerated sense of their intelligence and capabilities.

2. The covert or closet narcissist

They can also be called vulnerable narcissists because they don't fit the regular pattern of the typical narc. They are more passive-aggressive and can experience anxiety, depression, and low self-esteem. This makes them unable to receive criticism; they would rather avoid that scenario than be told off.

They may not exhibit the typical traits of narcissism, but they definitely possess the major narc characteristics. They can seem like saints, and they often associate with people that they admire. They also feel like they've been constantly victimized, and they're convinced that others are out to get them. They almost seem to feed off of the empathy and attention.

3. The toxic narcissist

This group of narcs can be described as "narcissism on steroids." They exist on the more severe end of the spectrum of toxicity and may exhibit other strongly negative traits like sadism, paranoia, and hostility. They have been described as the most dangerous type of narcissists because they will stop at nothing to achieve their goals even if it hurts the other person physically, mentally, emotionally, or financially.

4. The communal narcissist

This type of narc is all about being good and fair to others. They often have a high moral standard and are quick to fight against what they perceive to be injustice. The big problem here is that these types of narcissists are doing this for the social recognition and power that come with being a "freedom fighter." Another obvious discrepancy is the fact that their behavior often doesn't match up to their ideals under close scrutiny.

Which of these narcissists have you encountered before? Take a moment to examine your various relationships and evaluate them.

Codependent or Obsessive?

We all agree that humans need other humans and that "no man is an island." In fact, some level of vulnerability and dependence is encouraged when done in a healthy manner.

On the other hand, codependency comes into the picture when there is an unhealthy reliance on someone else. This behavior is born of low self-esteem, where the person who suffers from it comes to rely on an external source for validation.

This goes a step further than being a "people person" or being madly in love. A codependent individual has a hard time delineating their identity from the other person's. They don't know how to think for themselves or even what to feel about themselves, other people, and other situations. This comes about as a result of being raised in a dysfunctional environment with a lot of neglect and ignorance at play.

This lack of a strong sense of identity and an absence of self-love may translate into feelings of anxiety for the codependent individual, which makes them fixated on their relationships to distract themselves from the internal chaos.

The answer to the question above is that codependency and obsession often go hand-in-hand.

Am I Codependent?

The main theme of codependency is that the codependent individual puts other people's needs above their own. Now, it's essential to find out if you're a true romantic or if you're actually codependent.

Here are a few signs that may indicate you're codependent:

- You find it difficult to make decisions in your relationship.
- You don't trust yourself and you have low self-esteem.
- You're afraid of being abandoned.
- You don't pay any attention to your own needs or desires.
- You're always apologizing or taking the blame to avoid any drama.
- You're excessively worried about the other person's behaviors.
- You feel guilty whenever you do something for yourself alone.
- You always prefer to avoid conflict.
- You find yourself craving approval from other people.
- Your mood reflects other people's moods, not your own emotions.
- You try to control the other person's life or make decisions for them.

- You entertain fantasies about the other person and the state of your relationship with them, even if you're not fulfilled in the relationship.

When you find that your desire for your partner or loved one's wellbeing begins to cross the boundary into the unhealthy zone, then you need to step back and take a good look at what's happening.

Traits of Dependent Personality Disorder

Dependent personality disorder (DPD) is a mental health disorder that was first published in the Diagnostic and Statistical Manual of Mental Disorders, 3rd edition (DSM-III) in 1980. It was revised in 1987 (Ramsay & Jolayemi, 2020).

In the codependent individual, DPD causes a need for constant reassurance and an inability to have independent thoughts or make independent decisions without input from others. It's not unusual for this individual to feel helpless or even submissive to others. This behavior pattern is characterized by a lack of self confidence and fear of being alone.

According to the DSM-IV, a diagnosis of DPD can only be made when there is an overwhelming need to be cared for and if five of the following criteria are met (Ramsay & Jolayemi, 2020):

1. The individual cannot start projects by themselves because they lack self-confidence.

2. They agree with others even if they don't think they're right.

3. They do stuff that they don't like just so others will approve of them.

4. They don't like being alone and feel helpless when they're alone.

5. They allow other people to make important decisions for them.

6. They cannot make routine decisions without getting some form of reassurance from other people.

7. They are very afraid of being abandoned and are obsessed with preventing that outcome.

8. They are distressed when their intimate relationships come to an end and they quickly find someone to replace it.

If five of these eight criteria are satisfied, then we can boldly diagnose DPD. People with this condition are prone to self-criticism and may even stay away from big projects or commitments to avoid disappointing other people.

Signs You're in a Codependent Relationship

No matter how we may try to justify it—even if your partner indulges you or you're willing and able to indulge their tendencies and entertain their codependent needs—it's not a healthy state for any relationship to be in. While things may look rosy on the surface, the underlying issues that encompass low self-esteem, self-doubt, and fear of abandonment need to be worked on.

Guess what? Your codependent partner may be easy to live with now, but where does it stop? Can you guarantee that there won't be resentment and disappointment at some point? Can you truly promise to keep giving in to their demands and let them smother you?

Before we continue, let's look at some signs that you're in a codependent relationship:

Low self-esteem

The typical codependent often feels left out. It's possible that both people in this kind of relationship may suffer from poor self-esteem. Needing the other person's input and approval for basic decisions is a warning sign.

Absence of boundaries

There are bound to be problems with recognizing, acknowledging, and reinforcing boundaries in a codependent relationship. By their very definition, boundaries absolve you from being responsible for other people's happiness, which is what the codependent person needs to be. It's clear to see how boundaries will be shattered in such a relationship.

Tendency to people-please

Being a people-pleaser or being in a relationship with one can be quite frustrating. Most times, they don't even like what they're doing, but they feel obliged to continue so that they'll get the approval they seek. If your partner has this tendency or if you've been accused of this habit, you may need to pause and do some deep reflection.

More reactive than proactive to situations

Feeling obliged to take care of and please everyone else will cause a disconnect with your true wants and needs. This will hamper your ability to proactively navigate situations in a genuine manner and may keep you constantly on the defensive and even damage your self-esteem. It also doesn't help that you're not able to set proper boundaries as well.

Poor communication

Being a codependent person means that you're quick to disregard your own wants, and you may not express them even when you're aware of them. You may think that expressing yourself will just upset the other person and make them leave. On the flipside, a codependent person may not really understand their partner and may even enjoy the control they have, without taking time to listen to the other person.

It may be hard to identify a codependency cycle, break out of it, and stay out of it. However, it's important that you step away as soon as you can to examine the possible damage it has left on you as well as prevent future wounds.

Your Quick Workbook

This exercise aims to help you practice self-awareness, understand yourself better, and start making changes towards a healthier and happier life.

1. Write down 10 things you did for others within the past few days, both big and small.

_____

_____

_____

_____

_____

_____

2. Identify which of these actions were motivated by a desire to help the person, and which were motivated by a fear of rejection or abandonment.

_____

_____

_____

_____

_____

3. Identify in which of these actions you prioritized others above yourself.

_____

_____

_____

_____

_____

4. Write down 10 things that others have done for you within the last few days.

_____

_____

_____

_____

_____

5. Identify which of these actions are helpful and healthy, and which enable your codependency.

_____

_____

_____

_____

_____

6. Identify a specific relationship or situation in which you struggle with codependency.

_____

_____

_____

_____

_____

7. Describe your feelings, thoughts, and behaviors in this situation.

_____

_____

_____

_____

_____

8. What do you think are your underlying needs or fears in this situation?

_____

_____

_____

_____

---

9. How does your codependent behavior serve you in the short term?

_____

_____

_____

_____

_____

10. How does it harm you in the long term?

_____

_____

_____

_____

11. Write down what you want to change about your codependent behaviors.

_____

_____

_____

_____

_____

12. Write down a list of positive traits and values that you want to cultivate in yourself (e.g., self-care, self-respect, assertiveness, independence).

_____

_____

_____

_____

_____

13. Consider how you can start to develop and embody these positive traits and values in your life. This may include seeking therapy, engaging in self-reflection, setting boundaries with others, and seeking support from friends and family.

_____

_____

_____

_____

_____

Chapter 1 Takeaway

There are all sorts of humans on earth, and the fact is that a lot of us are not very good people. The narcissist is one of those not-really-good people, and identifying them isn't all that difficult. Dealing with them, however, is hard, and you must be ready for this.

Interdependence is the code of humanity. We can't do anything alone and will always need the help of others. But, just like with anything else in the world, abusing this principle even a bit will lead to a relationship where one person literally cannot do anything without the other (i.e., codependency). This is obviously not the best scenario, and things can get really dicey.

CHAPTER TWO

Narcissism-Codependency Dynamics

"Speaking the truth in love, may grow up in all things into Him who is the head—Christ."

—Ephesians 4:15 NKJV

"The narcissist devours people, consumes their output, and casts the empty, writhing shells aside."

— Sam Vaknin

A re narcissists drawn to codependent people? Is there a strange mechanism by which they connect? What's the big deal about narcissism and codependency anyways? Let's jump right in!

The Dance Between the Narcissist and the Codependent

Thus far we've taken a close look at the traits that accompany narcissism as well as those that are prominent in codependency.

In a nutshell, we could conclude that the codependent person is the giver in a relationship, willing to sacrifice their own happiness just so that their partner is happy. They're always taking care of others and seeing to other people's needs while ensuring that they get attention and reassurance from those people.

On the other side of the curtain, we have the narcissists, who I liken to black holes, ready to devour any and every crumb of attention and affection from others.

Both of these personality types have a few things in common, such as:

- They both need to stay in control.
- They both need attention and approval from other people.
- They both have poor self-esteem.
- They neither recognize nor respect boundaries set in relationships.

One major difference between the two is that narcs are very entitled and often lack empathy while codependents are not. The next big question is: Why are narcissists and codependents attracted to each other?

Great question. You see, the narcissist has what the codependent wants and vice versa. The narc is drawn to the codependent person because of their tendency and willingness to give everything they have and sacrifice all for their partner's pleasure. The narc enjoys this codependent personality because it's acceptable for them to dominate and control to their heart's desire. They are content being the center of the relationship and eat up every bit of attention from the codependent while asking for more.

The needy codependent is drawn to the first version of the narcissist they met. That version is usually very charming and affectionate. The narc showers them with both physical and emotional signs of love, fulfilling all the codependent individual's deepest desires. They also feel needed and are always available to stroke the narcissist's ego and serve as a sounding board for their grand plans and great fantasies. We can even go so far as to say that the narc's bad behavior is equally perfect for the codependent—it makes them feel even more secure and loved.

When these two start the dance, they're eager and excited because they seem to complement each other perfectly, and it's like they're a match made in heaven. As the dance progresses, however, their true nature begins to shine forth and the loving version of the narcissist goes away. This makes the codependent anxious, and they try harder to win back that first version, which feeds the narcissist more and encourages them to misbehave even more. Eventually, they both realize that they're not exactly happy in the relationship.

But because both of their needs are being met, they could be stuck in that toxic cycle for a long time until someone tries to get help. Yikes.

A Narcissist vs. a Codependent: Is One Better Than the Other?

If you had to pick a relationship with one, which would you pick? I bet you'd say a codependent person because they're said to be warm, loyal, and selfless. If we looked closer, though, we'd find that they hide their weak traits by trying to meet other people's needs as a means of gaining approval and acceptance. They also believe that they are ultimately responsible for whatever their partner says and does. They even downplay their own needs by pretending not to have any if asked.

The truth remains that narcissism and codependency have the same core problem, but they express their needs in different ways. They both have a damaged sense of self, and this is the fuel behind most of their actions. This means that, on average, they rely on others to create their identities and they really value other people's opinions.

Narcissists are focused entirely on themselves and may only care about others when it benefits them. So they need a regular source of praise, admiration, and attention to attend to their egos. This is the narcissistic supply, and it's what the average narcissist thrives on.

Codependents are so focused on other people that serving others soon becomes their identity. They may go as far as controlling other people because they're convinced that they know best for that person. Instead of praise, admiration, and attention, the codependent needs to be needed and loves to be thanked. In a way, you could say they're just as bad as narcs because they're focused on achieving their own goals and satisfying their needs at every point in time. It gets worse as time goes by because the codependent individual starts to believe they're the only one special or powerful enough to truly help the other people in their life.

The whole point I'm trying to make here is that it's not necessary to view narcissism and codependency as opposite sides of the scale. Instead, it's in our best interest to realize that both types of personalities are operating from a similar motivation and are trying to achieve the same thing, albeit through different methods.

This is why it's extremely possible to probe a codependent individual's behavior and find that they have some narcissistic traits and expectations that they simply express in a different manner. Instead of trying to consider which personality type is "better," think of their driving force and willingness to achieve their aims using different methods for a clearer view on the issue.

Can a Person Be Both Codependent and a Narcissist?

Since we've already established that narcissism and codependency have a common root and that they both depend on others for validation, it's not far fetched to wonder if narcissists can be codependents or if codependents can have a narcissistic personality (or, at the very least, narcissistic traits) too.

In life, I think you'll find that things are hardly ever clearly delineated in black and white. Most times, there are so many shades of gray that you may find yourself getting lost amidst all the grays. One thing that narcs and codependents often have in common is having experienced some form of abuse or trauma while growing up. Of course, having parents with NPD or who were codependent themselves also plays a huge role. Some might say they're two sides of the same coin, but sometimes the boundaries between the two conditions can get blurred and you find traits from one condition in the other.

It's not surprising to find that, in a relationship between a narc and a codependent person, the narcissist may try to manipulate their codependent partner into thinking that they're a narcissist themselves, just to control them. It's also not out of place to see codependent people exhibiting narcissistic traits from time to time.

A young lady I worked with, Kaley, once told me that she knew she was definitely codependent. In a stunning burst of insight, she also admitted that she had some narcissistic tendencies which came into play quite often. "I knowingly manipulated people into staying with me even though I made it look like I was vulnerable. Every time I went above and beyond to take care of them, I deliberately made sure they'd stay with me. It was a form of control for me and I got high off the fact that I could really make them do whatever I wanted."

- Thomas

Kaley was clearly codependent, with narcissistic traits she'd probably learned as a child.

It's also entirely possible for a narcissist to have codependent traits, but this doesn't mean they suddenly become nicer. Nope, this simply means they're more consumed with being admired, respected, and/or feared.

If you're having a hard time deciding whether someone you know is codependent or narcissistic, there is a likelihood that they are either codependent with narcissistic traits or a narcissist that is also codependent.

Behavioral Patterns and Characteristics of Codependency

Everyone is interdependent to a certain extent, and that's to be expected and even encouraged. It's hard to strictly define the specific behaviors that indicate codependency, but the main operating principle here is the law of reciprocity. This means that there's a form of healthy exchange, a give and take, that makes a relationship healthy. The burden of giving doesn't solely lie with one person; both partners give and receive based on who's in the most need at that particular time. This type of exchange exemplifies a healthy interdependent relationship.

There's no one-size-fits-all approach to identifying codependency because a codependent person may exhibit various patterns in response to their environment and their interactions with others. Here are some common patterns you need to be aware of:

They like to take control

This urge to control others is born from the belief that other people are simply not as capable of taking care of themselves. You'll find a codependent with this pattern trying to tell others what to do, or even how to think. They often offer unsolicited advice and can feel resentful if their offer of help isn't accepted.

They're not above giving extravagant gifts or doing people favors to influence them or gain approval. As is typical of most codependents, they need to feel needed by others. They may try to charm their way into being seen as caring, but sometimes they can be stubborn and uncooperative.

They exhibit avoidance patterns

They may be evasive in their communication just to avoid conflict. They may avoid people who might reject or shame them for their actions. They are prone to judging others harshly and will go as far as avoiding physical and emotional contact just to maintain distance. They pull others toward them only to push them away because they don't want to have intimate relationships. These types of codependents believe that expressing emotions is weak, and they never show appreciation.

They may be in denial

At this point, they can't really identify their feelings or they'd rather minimize their feelings. They are very conscious of the fact that they see themselves as generous and committed to other people's wellbeing. Most of them do not have empathy for other people's feelings, and they never see that the person to whom they're attached is not available or healthy for them.

They have poor self-esteem

Most codependents struggle with self-esteem, and this makes it difficult for them to make a decision on their own. They are quick to judge anything they say or do as inferior and do not think they deserve love or are special.

They also have a need to always appear to be correct and will go as far as lying to look good to others. They think they are better than others and may not easily admit to their mistakes. Of course, they aren't able to set proper boundaries and often run to other people for a sense of safety and security.

They may be extremely compliant

They are very loyal and don't mind staying in situations that aren't safe for them just to be close to others. They will easily compromise their own personal values and even their integrity as long as it's for others. They are also hyperaware of other people's feelings and can assume those feelings. They are quick to make decisions without thinking about the consequences, and they will accept special attention in place of love.

Which of these patterns are familiar to you?

Why You Should Deal with Narcissistic-Codependent Relationships Quickly

Narcissistic-codependent relationships can be incredibly damaging and toxic, and it's important to recognize when you're in one and take steps to address the issue. True, if you're codependent it may seem better to just stay put and manage your partner's harmful behaviors, but sooner or later you'll realize that this partnership is damaging you mentally, and you need to sit up and address this situation.

Another major thing to keep in mind is the fact that you're not really meeting the narcissist's needs. They aren't truly happy. So even if you feel like you're giving them your all and you're being appreciated for it, it'll get to the point where nothing you do will seem to be enough and they will never be happy. You must know that this isn't your fault because no one is capable of truly meeting their needs anyway. I compared a narcissist to a black hole earlier; that's because black holes are yawning abysses that devour everything without being affected—even whole planets and galaxies. Narcissists do the same to the people in their lives.

When these two types of people come together in a relationship, we already know that the narcissist is able to exploit the codependent's need to be needed, while the codependent is able to feed the narcissist's need for admiration and attention. This creates a cycle of manipulation and exploitation, with the codependent being constantly hurt and used, and the narcissist never getting their true needs met.

Recognizing the signs of a narcissistic-codependent relationship, such as feeling like you're constantly walking on eggshells, being constantly criticized and put down, and feeling like you're always giving more than you're getting in return, is essential.

I know it can be incredibly difficult to leave a codependent relationship with a narcissist. Narcissists can be charming and alluring at first, but their true colors often reveal themselves over time. They can be controlling, manipulative, and emotionally abusive. Apart from the damage to your self-esteem and mental health when they make you feel like you are not good enough, and their constant criticism and belittling of you, they will also gaslight you, making you question your own reality. This can lead to feelings of worthlessness, anxiety, and depression.

Of course, being codependent can prevent you from asserting your own needs and desires and can make it difficult for you to make decisions or to leave the relationship. Codependency can also lead to a lack of boundaries, which can further enable the narcissist's toxic behavior.

The first step in managing a narcissistic-codependent relationship is to recognize that you deserve better. You deserve to be in a relationship where you feel respected, valued, and loved. You deserve to be in a relationship where your needs are met and your feelings are taken into account. It's important to remind yourself that you are worthy of love and respect, and that you don't have to put up with being treated poorly.

The next step is to set boundaries with your partner. This means standing up for yourself and refusing to accept negative or abusive behavior. It also means setting limits on what you will tolerate in the relationship and communicating these boundaries clearly to your partner. This can be difficult, especially if you're used to putting the needs of your partner above your own, but it's important to remember that you deserve to be treated with respect and kindness.

It's also important to seek out support during this process. This can come in the form of friends, family, or a therapist. It's important to have people in your life who can support you and remind you of your worth, and who can help you navigate the difficult process.

Don't forget to focus on yourself and your own wellbeing. Take care of yourself physically, emotionally, and mentally. Engage in activities that make you happy and fulfilled, and surround yourself with positive and supportive people. It's also important to work on any personal issues that may have contributed to the relationship, such as low self-esteem or a need to be needed.

Your Quick Workbook

This exercise focuses on helping you reflect on the negative impacts of being in a narcissistic-codependent relationship and gain a clearer understanding of how harmful the relationship is.

1. Write down a list of behaviors and thoughts that are common in codependents as we discussed above, such as putting others' needs before their own, feeling responsible for others' emotions, difficulty setting boundaries, low self-esteem, and constantly seeking validation from others.

_____

_____

_____

_____

_____

2. Reflect on which of these behaviors and thoughts you recognize in yourself.

_____

_____

_____

_____

_____

3. Consider how these behaviors and thoughts have affected your own life, relationships, and wellbeing. For example, have you given up your own goals and desires in order to please others? Have you neglected your own emotional and physical needs?

_____

_____

_____

_____

_____

4. Identify patterns in your relationship: Take note of the behavioral patterns and dynamics in your relationship. How does your partner treat you and how do you respond?

_____

_____

_____

_____

_____

5. Write down all of the negative thoughts, feelings, and behaviors that you experience in the relationship. This can include things like low self-esteem, self-doubt, anger, anxiety, and depression.

_____

_____

_____

_____

_____

6. Reflect on how these negative experiences impact your life outside of the relationship. For example, do they interfere with your work, your relationships with friends and family, or your ability to engage in hobbies and activities you enjoy?

_____

_____

_____

_____

7. Write down all of the positive things about yourself that you have lost or given up in the relationship. This can include things like your self-worth, your confidence, your independence, and your ability to make decisions for yourself.

_____

_____

_____

_____

_____

Chapter Two Takeaway

Narcissistic-codependent relationships are very complicated, and finding yourself in the midst of such a relationship can be a bit disorienting. While the codependent might seem more of a mellow personality than the narcissist, both are toxic traits to have, and having relationships with such people will drain you more than it fills you.

Building Immunity Against the Weapons of a Narcissist

"For the grace of God has appeared, bringing salvation for all people, training us to renounce ungodliness and worldly passions, and to live self-controlled, upright, and godly lives in the present age."

—**Titus 2:11-12 ESV**

"When I look at narcissism through the vulnerability lens, I see the shame-based fear of being ordinary. I see the fear of never

feeling extraordinary enough to be noticed, to be lovable, to
belong, or to cultivate a sense of purpose."

—Brené Brown

One of the greatest Chinese generals to ever walk the earth, Sun Tzu, compiled his war strategies in a book titled *The Art of War*. Those war strategies have been modified into principles to arm readers in all fields with the required insight to be victorious in life. We all need strategies to subdue anything that threatens our peace and prosperity.

Well, consider the things I'm about to share with you to be the strategies you'll need to emerge victorious against the toxicity of a narcissist threatening your wellbeing. You're not literally in a war situation, but when you're in a toxic relationship with a narcissist, there will be more conflicts going on in your mind than there would be taking place on a literal battlefield.

Here are your strategies to win:

Understand How a Narcissist Thinks

Narcissists may use their physical appearance, charm, or intelligence to manipulate those around them. They usually target a specific group of people: empathetic, kind, and easily manipulated people. Narcissists can also be very persuasive, but their main goal is to maintain control and gain power over others.

The online resource *Abuse Warrior* explains that manipulation (a frequent tactic of narcissists) can be emotional or psychological. The goal of emotional manipulation is to make the victim lose their emotional stability. Psychological manipulation, on the other hand, affects the victim's mental capability to the point that the victim's beliefs or behaviors align with exactly what the manipulator wants.

These are a few ways narcissists manipulate:

Lying

Making a false statement and making it look like it's the truth. This could toy with the victim's mind and create confusion. The narcissist can make their victim look like a liar with a false statement.

Deflecting

When a narcissist is caught lying, they try to deflect the accusation to their victim; they make their victim look like the real culprit. They rarely take responsibility for their deceptive actions.

Stalking

A narcissist will make the extra effort to monitor their victim's movements, transactions, activities, etc., with the aim of knowing everything possible about their victim. This give them information with which to manipulate the person even more.

Other tactics include playing the victim, gaslighting, shifting the goalposts, projecting, and more. Next up, we'll dive into a few of these in depth and show you how to handle them.

Handling Guilt Tripping

A narcissist will do their best to make their victim doubt their ability to care, love, or show compassion for anyone. A narcissist does this by making statements that make their victim feel guilty about not being caring or loving enough, or for not showing enough compassion.

Threatening

This is one of the most potent weapons narcissists use. They use the tool of fear to subdue their victim by threatening them into submission.

Blaming

When the spotlight eventually shines on victims of any form of manipulation, they're made to look like they're responsible for what has been happening to them. A narcissist manipulates their victim in such a way that the victim will have defend their actions, thereby protecting the narc.

Know this: whenever someone tries to influence your feelings or your behavior to align with what they want, it's narcissistic. But how do you respond to this?

Your Strategy:

Dislodge fear

Fear is a terrible place to be. Once a narcissist manipulates you into a place of fear, it becomes easy for them to bend your mind and emotions to their will. The first step to combat this is to note down the things your manipulator does to instill fear in you. It's usually not the same for everyone. Identify yours.

Get the facts straight

Narcissists threaten their victims with false statements that could be used against the victim. What could be better as a way to prevent this than knowing the truth and being confident about it? There's a sense of security that comes with knowing the truth about something.

Set clear boundaries

This is what this book is about. You need to learn to set limits to how far you can allow a narcissist partner, colleague, or relative to intrude into your space.

Communicate your views assertively

Stay calm and composed. Don't be jittery or defensive. Just make your point and wait or move on as the occasion demands.

Handling Gaslighting

Interestingly, Merriam-Webster Dictionary voted the word "gaslighting" as 2022 Word of the Year because it was the most searched word. Wondering why lots of people searched for this word? Well, in my view, people were curious about the word due to the increase in its usage and, more importantly, increase in the experience.

According to research group YouGov, about 75% of adults in the U.S. knew nothing about this term in 2017, even though it has been in use since the 1930s (Bame, 2017). However, the experience has always been there. Sweet (2021) describes the gaslighting experience as a form of psychological abuse that makes victims feel they're crazy.

One of the victims of gaslighting Sweet interviewed explained that during her 12-year marriage, her ex-husband regularly cheated. But he would defend himself by calling her crazy and paranoid despite the evidence of his affairs she produced. She worked diligently to provide all the care her children needed on her own, but her ex-husband convinced her that she still needed him. One of the ways he did this was by delaying the payment of the electricity bills, and then waiting till the power was shut off. He would then blame her. The goal was to make her seem dependent on him despite her best efforts.

In other words, a narcissist tries to make you disbelieve what you know to be truth, thereby making you doubt your ability to know what truth is. When a narcissist wants to manipulate their victim, they make them question their sanity, memory, or perception of events. This can be done through lying, denying, or contradicting the victim's reality.

Ultimately, it'll cause the victim to doubt themselves and the people around them. The victim can become battered emotionally because it's a form of emotional abuse.

Your Strategy:

Acknowledge it

The first strategy to overcoming any form of abuse is to admit that it is happening to you. Failure to do this will mask the truth and, thus, the solution that could liberate you.

Stop doubting yourself

The whole point of gaslighting is to get you to distrust yourself and doubt your sanity. But the truth is that you're not insane. What you know about the issue is the truth. What you see isn't an illusion, and you aren't just making it up. It's true.

Detach yourself from other people's opinions

One of the ways you can stop doubting yourself is to detach yourself from other people's opinions about what is true. Don't argue with them. Just independently hold on to your truth and let it be the light that guides your action. You have the right to have your own thoughts and feelings. As a matter of fact, you're not insane. Don't let anyone drive you crazy regardless of the place they hold in your life. Your mental health is your priority.

Handling Love Bombing

Loving someone is a great thing, isn't it? It's certainly not a bad thing to demonstrate to someone how much you love them. However, there's a point when this demonstration of love is taken to the extreme. That's when it becomes manipulative. That's the point when love becomes love bombing. Don't get me wrong; people can show love excessively for genuine reasons too. However, there are those whose motive is to manipulate the recipient of their love.

Love bombing is a manipulative tactic that can be employed in romantic and non-romantic relationships. The strategy is the same in both contexts. A narcissist "bombs" someone with love to win over and control the other person. They achieve this by showering them with excessive attention, affection, and gifts.

The goal is to create a sense of dependency and make it difficult for the other person to see the need to set boundaries. Peykar (cited by Lamothe, 2019) notes that a narcissist who showers you with excessive love typically has a goal. Once they win your trust and affection, they can carry on with their plan.

Love bombing could be mistaken for genuine love because the signs are similar, but pay attention to these love bombing signals:

- They lavish you with gifts that you cannot decline because you'll be in their black book if you do.

- They give you extravagant compliments that make your head spin.

- They demand all your attention and time to the point that you may be isolated from your family and friends. When your supposed lover gets angry that you made plans to spend time with someone else instead of with them, that's a love bombing red flag.

- They persuade you to make an early commitment to a long-term relationship.

Your Strategy:

- Don't neglect the inner feelings of sadness when you're isolated from other people besides your lover. Or the feeling that something's wrong when you constantly get unnecessary gifts, or when they suggest starting a committed relationship very early on.

- Don't be sentimental. Go in with your eyes open. Don't make rash decisions based on how you feel at that moment. Give it time. It's easier to opt out when you've not made a long-term commitment than when you've gone all-in.

- Note the red flag if you feel suffocated by your partner's fast-paced demands to be in a committed relationship almost immediately, or that you always be available whenever they need you without consideration for your needs.

Handling Triangulation

One of the things you should always remember about a narcissist is that they're toxic players who derive joy from watching other people get frustrated and disoriented. One of the strategies they employ to achieve this is triangulation.

This is a manipulative tactic that a narcissist may use to control and manipulate their relationships. The narcissist involves a third person in the relationship in order to make the other person jealous or to create a sense of competition. The narcissist may use triangulation to create feelings of insecurity in their partner, to control their partner's behavior, or to create a sense of dependence on the narcissist. Narcissistic triangulation can be emotionally damaging to all parties involved and can lead to the breakdown of relationships.

Here's a good example of triangulation:

Will and Anna had been seeing each other for a few months. Will showered Anna with lots of affection, attention, and gifts (love bombing). That was enough for Anna to fall madly in love with Will. After all, that's exactly what he wanted. They began to talk about marriage and babies. Will kept assuring her that he loved her and she was perfect for him.

At some point, Anna started noticing that the loads of texts from Will were no longer flooding her phone as usual. He kept evading her questions. He started finding fault with her over trivial issues.

Before long, Anna found out that Will was seeing another girl, Lindsay. Will started comparing Anna with Lindsay. It hurt her feelings. She expressed this to Will, but he said she was just being jealous and that there was nothing to worry about. Yet he was doing this deliberately to stir up jealousy in Anna—and he was doing the same thing to Lindsay.

As a result, the two women began to envy each other. Will was enjoying the little show he had set up and the attention he was getting from it. The entire scenario fueled his need to control the situation.

Your Strategy:
Recognize triangulation

If you've not noticed it yet in your relationship, you might need to take a closer look and assess the pattern of interaction. If you discover that you're being pulled into a triangle dynamic, you must begin to handle the situation maturely. Use the following strategies:

- Review your interactions with people who triangulate you.

- Don't get stuck in the circle of manipulation.

- Don't get drawn into silly competitions with anyone. Focus on yourself and your life.

- Don't get carried away with positive compliments that compare you with another person.

- Safeguard your emotional wellbeing by hanging around a network of healthy friends.

- Stop sharing personal details with anyone that draws you into a triangle dynamic.

Handling Playing the Victim

Playing the victim is another strategy narcissists employ to manipulate their victim. No one would expect a narcissist to play the victim card because they're egoistic and love to be in control. But if playing the victim card gives them an opportunity to manipulate their victim, why wouldn't they?

Playing the victim card is nothing new to most of us, though. At times, non-narcissists do this too. When someone wants to get sympathy and make other people feel like they're responsible for their predicament, that's playing the victim card. People who play the victim card don't ever want to take responsibility for the negative things that happen to them. They cry and indulge in self-pity to make other people feel like they're the reason for it.

It might not be an intentional or regular thing for a non-narcissist, but a narcissist uses it as a weapon against their victim. This is manipulative. It pushes the victim into a position of helplessness, where they feel mentally stressed and unable to fight back against the layers of lies cast on them.

Casabianca (2021) suggests that a narcissist feels attacked when you don't agree with them or when you point out their mistake. Their inability to introspect and their inflated self-worth prevents them from seeing the situation as they ought to. Therefore, they resort to playing the victim card in some scenarios.

Why should you feel guilty for the mistakes of someone else?

Your Strategy:

- Don't ever doubt yourself.

- Don't take a narcissist's words to heart. Try not to pay attention to them.

- When you see the sign, don't take the bait. Control your need to respond or defend yourself and just walk away.

- Don't go along with their pity party. It only boosts their ego.

Handling Projections

If you've ever had a relationship with a narcissist, you'll know that generally they lack self-awareness. They derive their sense of self-esteem and self-worth from other people's perceptions of them. They don't believe they have any flaws, and they never accept they are wrong about anything. When fingers are pointed at them, they blame it on other people.

Their shortcomings, mistakes, and misfortunes never seem to be their fault. There is always someone to blame for it. This is a manipulative strategy called projection.

Cikanavicius (2019) identifies a few ways narcissists project and attack their victim. These include:

1. Calling you things that you are not

When they're the real culprit, they tend to loudly accuse you of the things they are guilty of. For instance, they may say you're cheating on them when, in actuality, they're the one cheating on you. They may accuse you of only ever thinking about yourself while in the meantime they're the truly selfish person in the relationship, never showing empathy for anyone else. It's just always about them.

2. Grandiosity, mimicking, and exaggeration

Here's how a narcissist thinks: "I'm special and deserve exceptional treatment. Everyone else must see how special I am and treat me specially. No one else matters here more than I do." This is the type of thinking that makes them feel entitled and better than everyone else.

They have a distorted perception of the world and themselves. Therefore, when they manipulate other people through lies, gaslighting, projection, exploitation, and other manipulative tactics to boost their self-esteem and satisfy their egoistic needs, they see it as a normal thing.

At other times, to make themselves seen and recognized by everyone, they take on other people's traits and achievements out of envy. They can mimic, defame, and belittle others, and/or destroy other people's credibility, to assert themselves.

According to Cikanavicius (2019), narcissists also play the victim in projecting.

How can you respond to this?

Just as with other manipulative strategies, don't ever doubt yourself and don't let your emotions get the best of you.

Handling Smear Campaigns

Another dangerous manipulative trick of a narcissist is a smear campaign. It's a step further from playing the victim card. When a narcissist discovers that they've been exposed, they go on a campaign to put their victim on the spot by damaging their victim's reputation among their friends and family. The narcissist acts fast to make themselves appear to be the victim rather than a vicious monster.

When a narcissist goes on a smear campaign, they're out to paint their victim as insane, an addict, an alcoholic, unstable, a thief, a cheater, or a poor parent. They achieve this by falsifying and exaggerating their victim's conduct. The goal is to destroy the victim's credibility and sanity.

How will this turn out for the victim? The victim will have no one to run to since their image has been tarnished among their support system. They'll feel isolated, unsure about their sanity, and helpless.

Your Strategy:

- Don't respond to the accusations with an outburst of anger. Try to be calm.

- Know your truth. Even if the whole world stands against you, don't stand against yourself.

- Don't post anything on an online public space or social media to defend yourself. A narcissist will use it against you.

- Set a limit to how much they can intrude into your space.

- Speak with only a trusted circle of friends and tell them your side of the story.

The best way to gain an advantage over a narcissist is to think the way they think and set up strategies to counter their moves whenever possible.

Your Quick Workbook

1. Identify triggers: Write down what specifically triggers you when interacting with the narcissistic person. How can you anticipate these triggers and prepare yourself emotionally?

_____

_____

_____

_____

_____

2. Practice self-awareness: Write down ways you can increase self-awareness and recognize when you are becoming emotionally involved in the narcissistic person's drama. What techniques can you use to shift your focus back to yourself? (This could be a breathing exercise, or body scanning where you focus your attention on each part of your body, often from your head to your toes.)

_____

_____

_____

_____

_____

3. Limit exposure: Write down specific steps you can take to limit your exposure to the narcissistic person. How will you maintain your emotional detachment in their presence?

_____

_____

_____

_____

_____

4. Focus on self-care: Write down specific self-care practices you can implement to support your wellbeing. How will you prioritize self-care in your daily routine?

_____

_____

_____

_____

_____

5. Seek support: Write down specific individuals (friends or family members) you can reach out to for support. How will you maintain your support network and ensure they are aware of your situation?

_____

_____

_____

_____

_____

6. Challenge negative beliefs: Write down the negative beliefs and thought patterns that may make it difficult to emotionally detach from the narcissistic person. How will you replace these negative beliefs with positive, empowering ones?

_____

_____

_____

_____

7. Visualize a positive outcome: Write down how you want the situation with the narcissistic person to be resolved. What would be your ideal outcome and how will you visualize this outcome to maintain emotional detachment?

_____

_____

_____

_____

Chapter Three Takeaway

A wise man once said, "Know thy enemy." And make no mistake, narcissists are your enemy. They have several tactics that they use, consciously or unconsciously, to manipulate you and get you exactly where they want you. And as you can guess, that's not where you want to be.

Understanding these tactics is key to remaining a step ahead in your dealings with them.

Detoxification From Toxic Relationships

"Above all else, guard your heart, for everything you do flows from it."

—Prov. 4:23 (NIV)

"I can be changed by what happens to me, but I refuse to be reduced by it."

—Maya Angelou

Understanding the Six Relationship Types and Their Impact on Your Life

Have you ever had a great relationship with someone without knowing that person's place in your life?

It's important you pay attention to this. If you intend to set boundaries for certain forms of relationships, it's crucial you understand the relationships in your life and know the purpose and function of each. It's true that every relationship serves a purpose. But not all relationships are the same. For instance, your relationship with your partner can't be compared with your relationship with the lady who works at the grocery store down the street. They're different, but all are important.

Each relationship is meant to serve a unique purpose in your life, but no relationship can give you everything you need in life. The moment you understand this, you'll save yourself a lot of trouble in assuming every relationship is supposed to give you the same result. Through this, you can also identify which relationships to hold dear and which to let go.

Before I show you different types of relationships, try to understand that when you comprehend and correctly identify every relationship in your life, communication becomes effective, and problem-solving and decision-making in your relationships becomes easy. You'll be able to interact with everyone around you in meaningful ways.

So, here we go:

1. Family Relationships

For most people, the first type of relationship they experience is relationship with the people they're related to by blood. It's only in certain circumstances that people grow up outside a family system. However, from birth, a child begins to get acquainted with a certain culture, customs, and beliefs within the family setting. This implies that the family is the first foundational institution that shapes our minds and the way we see the world.

Although not all family relationships are positive, the cord that binds you to your family makes it hard to sever relationships with them. If a person experiences narcissism or codependency in the family, the relational bond remains intact, but their mind has been shaped to accept toxicity in relationships as a norm. This makes family relationships unique and different from every other relationship.

2. Friendships

Think of living on earth without friends. What do you think that'd look like? Probably not too good. Friends make the world go round, right? I consider friendship to be the next foundational type of relationship after family.

Most people begin having friends in childhood, either from their neighborhood, at school, or at their place of worship. According to an article from the Exchange Family Center (2019), the friends most people start keeping from childhood create in them a sense of belonging and security. This also contributes to the quality of life a person goes on to live.

There are different types of friends. Some are just acquaintances, others are social friends, and most people have a few intimate ones. Each of these friends has a place in our lives. The way a person is treated within a circle of friends influences their perception of themselves, their self-esteem, and ultimately their effectiveness in society.

When you understand the level of friendship you have with someone, you'll be able to determine how much they can influence you.

3. Social Relationships

Social relationships cover the relationships you have with your coworkers, distant relatives, and neighbors. We all have people we work with professionally in some capacity, either remotely or onsite. Our relationships with coworkers are usually at a different level from the ones we have with our family or friends; however, professional relationships determine our productivity.

An article from Mind Tools observes that the more comfortable colleagues are with each other, the more confident they'll feel to voice their opinions, share a workspace, and jump on innovative ideas. This fosters group morale and productivity.

Good work relationships allow you to focus on opportunities for personal development and to win new business and enhance your career. A negative work environment due to poor relationships, conversely, will demoralize you and affect productivity.

4. Romantic Relationships

Primarily, this type of relationship grows out of friendship. A romance starts when the level of communication with someone grows from casual to intimate. It's at this point you begin to admit that you're in love.

The person you claim to be in love with has more access to you than just a casual friend or even someone you call your best friend. Therefore, your romantic partner has a lot of influence over your emotional and psychological wellbeing. This romantic partner can also influence your perception of yourself because you'll easily believe anything they say about you.

A romantic relationship is a strong form of relationship. If you're in a romantic relationship with someone toxic, you're in for some bad moments. A toxic romantic partner will take advantage of your vulnerability and use it against you.

5. Marital Relationships

Usually, a romantic relationship, if sustained, leads to a marital commitment between two lovers. They reproduce and raise a family. Some just choose to remain as partners, but this can still be categorized as a marital relationship.

A marital relationship requires another level of commitment and responsibility that makes you not only responsible for yourself, but for your partner as well. You can no longer just think about yourself alone; you have to think about your partner. You're not only in it for the special benefits of a marital relationship, but you're committed to living a purposeful life of meaning together.

A marital relationship means making a deliberate decision to go on a lifelong journey with your romantic partner. You'll have to be flexible enough to cope and live with your partner. Once this relationship goes wrong at the level of friendship, it'll be wrong at every other level. So, before you allow your relationship to grow past the phase of friendship, be sure you want to go further in that relationship with the person you're beginning to develop funny feelings for. If you aren't sure about their character, draw a line immediately!

6. Spiritual Relationships

Walton (1996) notes that a spiritual relationship involves the connection you have with yourself, other people, nature, and God at the soul level. He further states that all relationships can be spiritual. The depth of this kind of relationship is directly related to one's personal acceptance of the existence of the inner self.

The moment you begin to accept that there's more to you than your physique, your perception of yourself and the world around you will begin to change. Spending daily time with God will strengthen the true foundation of your life—because if there's a spiritual side to you, then there's a spiritual side to the world around you as well. That's the only way you can connect at that level with the world around you.

This kind of relationship will open you up to the possibility of exploring the fullness of your being and reality. If well cultivated, it'll take you beyond the realm of anxiety and lead you to a place of rest and peace.

Signs You're in a Toxic Relationship

Relationships are a neutral institution. They are neither good nor bad. It's the individuals involved that determine the type of relationship it will be.

How can you tell whether your relationship is unhealthy? When you begin to see the signs listed below, it's an indication that you're in a toxic relationship.

- You don't seem to do anything right anymore
- You're not feeling happy anymore

- You're feeling disrespected
- Every argument and disagreement is an opportunity to dig up the past
- Your needs are not met
- Communication is strained
- You're stuck in the euphoria of the past
- The excitement of the relationship is being replaced with blame and complaints
- There's no productive discussion about the future
- You're feeling choked in the relationship
- You're beginning to resent your partner
- You're beginning to lose friends
- There's no balanced commitment in the relationship
- You're giving more and getting little
- You're feeling undervalued
- It feels like you go from one criticism to another
- You can no longer raise your head with high self-esteem
- You're usually scared to air your views
- You're feeling unsupported
- You're losing faith in your partner's credibility
- You're losing peace over trivial issues
- You're feeling depressed

- You're seeing only each other's bad qualities

- You're feeling your worth comes from what your partner thinks of you

- You're feeling your opinion comes second to your partner's

- You're not feeling free around your partner

- You're feeling manipulated

- You're feeling used

- You're feeling inferior to your partner

- You're feeling unworthy

- You don't feel emotionally or mentally sound around your partner

- You're feeling lonely when you're together with your partner

- You find it hard to trust your partner

- You feel you're responsible for their happiness

- You're being abused physically or verbally or both

- You're being mocked regularly

- You're not being appreciated for your effort

- You don't spend time together anymore

- Your suggestions are usually turned down

- You've lost your privacy

- You're being stalked
- You've lost your sense of self-worth

All these and many others that are not listed here are signs of a toxic relationship. Assess your relationship to check if any of these symptoms are present.

Six Main Types of Toxic People

Just as we have good and loving people in our society, there are also toxic people. Toxic people are numerous, and you can find them anywhere, even in the most religious corners of society. Here, I'll focus on six toxic people groups.

Be careful of these groups of people:

Manipulators

A manipulator will always make plans to control you for their own benefit. They do this without any regard for how you feel or what happens to you. They're only interested in getting their needs met.

Narcissists are in this category. They take advantage of you and leave you psychologically and emotionally wounded.

Pessimists

These sets of people always have their heads down. Their natural outlook on life is negative. They don't see anything good about anything around them. The best they can see is the worst in every situation.

The terrible thing about this group of people is that they are influencers. They're usually quick to register their negative opinions about a project or any step forward. So, they instill fear in their friends or partner about whatever that step forward may be.

If you hang around these types of people, you'll quickly give up on your dreams and never become the best version of yourself.

Talebearers

A talebearer doesn't have a closed mouth. They're only interested in sharing juicy news. They're not interested in the good news; primarily, they're interested in the faults, failures, setbacks, and downfalls of other people. They're quick to spread such news.

Spreading this kind of information could cause discord between friends and, sometimes, irreparable damage in relationships.

People Pleasers

People pleasers are only interested in being in your good book. Even if you're going down the wrong path, they won't tell you the truth you need to hear because they don't want to hurt you.

People pleasers have low self-esteem, and they derive their worth from what you think of them.

If you're trying to get your self-esteem up, associating with a people pleaser won't help you achieve that. They'll only encourage you that it's okay to feel low and inferior to others.

Judgers

Judgmental people are quick to put on their critic's lens to nail you to the cross. When what you're doing doesn't seem good to them, they don't think about how they can learn from it. They just criticize it immediately.

Things are only good as far as their lens sees it as good. They have a way of squashing your passion if they don't like it, thus stifling your desire to be passionate and expressive. They make you feel terrible about yourself and what you intend to do. They rarely appreciate or commend people for the effort they put into something.

If you associate with these types of people, you'll dampen your self-worth and never see anything good about yourself.

What Being in a Toxic Relationship Does to You

A toxic relationship is poisonous to your emotional and psychological wellbeing. I have identified a few effects a toxic relationship could have on you:

1. Loss of self

The first significant effect a toxic relationship has is that you lose a sense of who you are. This is the most crucial part of anyone. Once you begin to lose sight of who you are, it becomes difficult to do anything meaningful with your life because a sense of identity is what gives your life direction and meaning. Your vision and ambition ought to align with your identity. If identity is lost, purposeful living is also gone.

A toxic relationship gradually kills that sense of identity. If such a relationship persists for a long time, you might lose it altogether.

2. Low self-esteem and self-worth

The way other people treat us tells us a lot about ourselves. If you're in a toxic relationship where the other person doesn't care about you, you're denied love and support, you're constantly abused—verbally and emotionally—and you're always ignored, it'll take a lot of self-talk not to feel bad about yourself. Your first natural response emotionally and psychologically would be to think less of yourself.

While in a toxic relationship, chances are you'll lose the confidence to ever speak up and try something innovative, and you'll stop believing in yourself.

3. Stunted personal growth

Being trapped in a toxic relationship doesn't allow room for personal growth and development. When you're not even in control of your life anymore, how could you think about pursuing any form of advancement? It's your partner that decides how far you'll go or what you can do.

When they do things to convince you that you're not good enough, and they constantly remind you of your past mistakes and downfalls, you'll not bother to attempt anything progressive.

Other effects could include:

- Decline in your physical, emotional, and psychological wellbeing
- Distorted perception of a healthy relationship
- Anxiety and perpetual fear

These and many more are the effects a toxic relationship could have on you.

Your Quick Workbook

1. Identify the toxic behaviors: Write down the specific behaviors or actions that are causing harm in the relationship.

_____

_____

_____

_____

_____

2. Evaluate the impact: How are these toxic behaviors affecting your mental and emotional wellbeing?

_____

_____

_____

_____

3. Consider your options: Brainstorm different options for addressing the situation, such as seeking therapy or setting boundaries. Which option are you going for?

_____

_____

_____

_____

_____

4. Prioritize self-care: Make a list of activities that bring you joy and peace and make time for them in your schedule. (Being in a toxic relationship is so depleting, you need to rejuvenate.)

_____

_____

_____

_____

_____

Chapter Four Takeaway

Once you've identified that you're in a toxic relationship, understand that you're in a sinking ship and the best way to survive it is to address the situation.

Overcoming Narcissism and Codependency in Origin Families

"Do you see a man hasty in his words? There is more hope for a fool than for him."

—Proverbs 29:20 (NKJV)

"It's not your job to manage the emotions of others. It's an exhausting role that may offer temporary bursts of self-worth, but ultimately will drain the life out of you."

—Jackson MacKenzie

The Enmeshed Family System and How it Works

One big happy family?

Meh. A sham.

Think again.

One of the reasons why Mel had a hard time admitting that her relationship with her mom was weird was because of the word "enmeshed." She said it sounded like she was a fly or maybe a fish trapped in a net, and that didn't sound pleasant at all.

As vivid an image as that conjures, I'd say that it's a pretty good definition of the concept. An enmeshed family is one where the members are so close-knit and reliant on each other that the natural boundaries and roles are blurred.

It wouldn't be hard to find the parents being overly reliant on their children for emotional support in such a setting, and the children not being allowed independence from their parents emotionally. People from enmeshed families tend to think that they're just super connected, but on close examination, a lack of boundaries gives the whole jig away.

This family system is dysfunctional and has damaging effects on both the children and the parents. It's easy to mistake a close family unit for an enmeshed one, but the difference lies in the fact that boundaries are in place in a healthy family. Once family members start to view non-family members as outsiders, it's a pretty good sign that it may be an enmeshed family.

A child from an enmeshed family doesn't have an identity separate from that of their parents or other family members. They don't think about their needs or place any importance on said needs, instead aligning their goals with what their parents want or what's best for the family.

They typically feel guilty for wanting some space from their family, and they are often bad at resolving conflict. You may find someone like that saying yes to things they don't really want just to avoid disappointing someone else. Another strong characteristic is the fact that they feel obliged to solve any problems that their family members may have, even when it's not directly theirs to solve.

Parents in an enmeshed family typically center their lives on their children and believe they can provide all the support and love their children need forever. This leads them to monitor their children's relationships with outsiders and dissuade them from getting too close to others. They expect their children to be like them, even down to having the same dreams, so naturally they prevent their child from trying to achieve their dreams, especially when it's not in line with what they want.

Children from an enmeshed family tend to have low self-esteem and fall into codependent relationships just because they're used to it.

Let's look at the individual interactions you'd see in this kind of setting.

Dealing with Narcissistic Siblings

We all know that growing up with siblings may be more of an obstacle course than a walk in the park, but have you considered the possibility that your difficult brother or sister may just be a narcissist?

Now, it's entirely possible that this sibling is not a narcissist but may have a few narcissistic traits that make getting along with them a herculean task. Either way, identifying these traits for what they are will teach you how to manage this relationship.

You probably haven't realized it yet, but growing up with a narcissistic sibling could be responsible for some of your character traits (usually negative ones) and has a profound effect on your mental health too. You may be used to avoiding that particular sibling or just resigning yourself to their manipulative behavior, and while you think you've survived just fine all this time, the impact of this relationship on you may very well extend to your other relationships and even other aspects of your life.

Having a toxic sibling makes you naturally distrustful of people. This is most likely because you've been deceived and manipulated by your toxic sibling. One minute you're best friends, the next they may do something to indicate that they never cared for you in the first place, and eventually you'll become hardened and distrusting.

You may also find out that you're willing to tolerate abusive relationships with others simply because you're used to enduring your toxic sibling's manipulation. If you're the type that's quick to make excuses for other people's behavior towards you, it's possible that you have accepted the fact that abuse is an inevitable part of every relationship thanks to the toxic narc in your life.

The incredible thing about narc siblings is that they're able to seem like innocent angels to your parents. In fact, they may enjoy painting you as the scapegoat of the family. They often position themselves as the model child who always does the right thing, which means confiding in your parents may be out of the picture. Naturally, you'll also find that you're almost deathly afraid of confrontations and any other kind of conflict, so you'll go the extra mile to avoid it.

Narcissists, as we know, hate criticism and often react dramatically to it. Being subjected to this dramatic performance over and over again will make you eager to avoid it as much as possible. That's probably why you roll over and give in to your narc sibling's desires, even when you'd rather not.

This behavior will be echoed in your other relationships— friendships, work relationships, and with romantic partners. It may even be so bad that you end up with a narc partner simply because that's what you're used to.

If you're used to being the one that other people run to for help or advice, there's a great possibility that you're not getting the same comfort from your friends. This is because you find yourself drawn to being the helper or confidant in most relationships. This may be because you're able to empathize with others better than the average person. It may even be because you're seeking to have the relationship you'd want with your siblings elsewhere, but you're not capable of trusting anyone else that much.

I think we can both agree that the effects of putting up with a toxic sibling spread farther than you may have originally imagined. If you have a sibling that's:

- Really cruel to you and seems to enjoy hurting you, whether physically, mentally, or emotionally;
- So toxic that you feel relief whenever you're not with them or in contact with them;
- Self-centered and makes everything about them;
- Excessively entitled even though they never reciprocate your efforts;
- Always portraying themselves as the good child while you're the black sheep; or
- Always striving to be in the limelight, even when it has nothing to do with them,

You most likely have a narcissistic sibling. So, how can you handle them? Here are a few steps to take:

Take back your self-confidence and self esteem

We can both agree that your self esteem will have taken a hit after putting up with a toxic person for so long. It can be hard to see yourself as someone other than whoever they've led you to believe you are. Taking the time out to destroy those negative notions about yourself is a crucial first step to breaking free of that toxic bondage. Spending more time with people who love and appreciate you goes a long way as well as affirming yourself as much as possible.

Set boundaries

This can look like choosing to walk away when they say hurtful things, refusing to engage when they're trying to bait you, informing them firmly that you'd prefer that they stop doing something you don't like, or even limiting your contact with them if need be. The hard work lies in cataloging their harmful behaviors and agreeing on what you don't want. Then you need to inform them of your new preferences and attach a condition to when they step out of bounds.

Enforcing these conditions may initially be challenging, but it's entirely possible.

Ultimately, focusing on self-care and being kind to yourself are important aspects of coping with a narcissistic sibling.

Codependent Siblings

Codependent siblings, like other codependent people, struggle with self-esteem and inferiority problems. Their selflessness usually hides a need to be in control and get validation or attention as a result.

Unfortunately, this affects both you and the codependent sibling because it puts the responsibility of making them happy solely on you. It also compels you to act a certain way to please them, even when you don't want to. It may also be enabling bad behavior and teaching you that you don't need to take care of yourself. As a result, you may turn out to be resentful and irresponsible.

It's important to set the right boundaries and stand by them. Prepare yourself for the fallout when you set these boundaries and steel yourself against the inevitable manipulation that's sure to follow.

You also need to work on your self-care practices. It's essential that you take care of yourself, and this includes taking responsibility for your feelings and actions. Taking the bold step to end your sibling's codependency can be tough, and you may even require help from others, but it's worth it in the end.

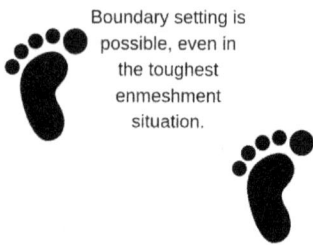

Boundary setting is possible, even in the toughest enmeshment situation.

Your Quick Workbook

1. Identify your boundaries:

    a. Write down your personal values, beliefs, and boundaries.

_____

_____

_____

_____

_____

b. Reflect on how they have been affected by the enmeshment in your family.

_____

_____

_____

_____

c. Identify what changes you need to make to assert your boundaries.

_____

_____

_____

_____

2. Assess the impact:

a. Reflect on how your family's enmeshment has affected your life and relationships.

_____

_____

_____

_____

_____

b. Write down the specific behaviors and patterns you need to change to break free.

_____

_____

_____

_____

_____

3. Set healthy boundaries:

a. Write down the specific steps you need to take to establish healthy boundaries with your family, including the narcissistic family member.

_____

_____

_____

_____

b. Identify what you are willing and not willing to tolerate in your relationships.

_____

_____

_____

_____

4. Communicate your boundaries:

a. Plan a conversation with your family about your new boundaries and what you need from them.

_____

_____

_____

_____

b. Practice the conversation in your mind or with a trusted friend.

c. Be clear, direct, and assertive when speaking with your family, including the narcissistic member.

5. Break the cycle of codependency:

a. Identify your codependent tendencies and work on breaking the cycle.

_____

_____

_____

_____

b. Practice self-care and self-love to reduce codependent behaviors.

6. Keep reassessing:

a. Regularly check in with yourself to see if your boundaries are being respected.

b. Make any necessary adjustments to ensure that your boundaries remain intact.

c. Celebrate your progress and growth.

Managing an enmeshed family system is a challenging but rewarding journey. With clear boundaries, self-care, and support, you can create a healthier and happier life.

Chapter Five Takeaway

Blood is thicker than water, the popular saying goes. But is it thicker than toxicity? I don't think so. Dealing with narcissists is one thing, but dealing with narcissists who are also family members is something different. It can often make you feel closed in with nowhere to go, and because they are family, you may often feel like it's your responsibility to fix them.

Big mistake.

You can't change anyone who doesn't want to change. It's that simple. With codependent and/or narcissistic family members, it's best to learn how to use boundaries to manage your interactions with them.

CHAPTER SIX

Tips for Setting Healthy Boundaries

"Wounds from a friend can be trusted, but an enemy multiplies kisses."

—Proverbs 27:6

"Lack of boundaries invites lack of respect."

—Anonymous

Have you ever lived on a ranch before? Or perhaps you've visited one? If you have, one thing you'll realize is that, while the ranch hands have a variety of duties to attend to every day, there's always someone whose job is to go inspect the fence line for any damages and repair it at once.

That can be very tasking, especially if the ranch is a large one. It may require that the ranch hand ride for long distances simply to maintain the border, yet it's so important to the wellbeing of the ranch that someone's always assigned to this duty, come rain, come snow, or come shine. Keeping the border intact keeps the precious cattle in and prevents outsiders from sneaking into the ranch and causing havoc.

This is a great example of what setting boundaries looks like. Everyone talks about the great step you need to take to set your boundaries, but less emphasis is placed on its maintenance. This is a common mistake, and I tell anyone who cares to listen that maintaining and updating your boundaries is at least as important as setting them up.

Why You Need to Set Boundaries

Take it from me when I say that boundaries make a whole world of difference. The difference between having balanced relationships with the people in your life and being a people pleaser or always muddled up in obligations you don't want (eventually hating your life as a result) lies in your boundaries.

Yep. You heard me right. If you hate your life, you may need to examine your boundaries to see what you're letting in that's stealing your peace. Setting boundaries helps you to:

Be more confident about your needs

Realizing what you need and asserting these needs to others is a very crucial benefit of setting boundaries. This means that you have no choice but to evaluate what you need and how you feel. The very act of standing for what you want will permeate other aspects of your life, teach you how to be more assertive, and improve all areas of your life.

Meet your needs

How many times have your needs gone unmet in a relationship? Have you quietly accepted the fact that your needs aren't really important? If so, you need to start setting boundaries yesterday! This will help you recognize that your needs are valid and also get them met, be it by you or by others.

Get more time and energy

The fact that the opportunity cost of doing stuff for other people means you have less time and energy to do what makes you really happy should be a huge motivating factor for you to set those boundaries. You'll also be less angry and resentful because you won't be doing things that either waste your time or go against your values. I mean, would you choose to do stuff that weighs you down or stuff that fills you up and makes you happy? It's a no-brainer, right?

Be more compassionate

Being firm about your boundaries doesn't mean that you're wicked or selfish. Feeling guilty about setting boundaries doesn't mean that it's wrong to do so, either; it just means you've taught yourself not to ask for what you need because you think you don't matter. Putting up those boundary lines is a great way of respectfully communicating your needs to others. In respecting your boundaries, they also learn to respect and value themselves.

Stay protected

What if you didn't have to deal with the drama of your narc partner or codependent siblings? Think how much clearer your mind would be and how much your anxiety would lessen. Boundaries act as a shield against messy situations, physical violence, unwanted feelings, and even self-criticism.

Myths Holding You Back From Setting Healthy Boundaries

What are your worst fears about setting boundaries? A lot of people I've spoken to say that they don't want to set boundaries for a number of reasons, usually based on misconceptions they have about boundaries.

We've seen what boundaries are and why it's important to set them; now let's look at what they're **not**.

They don't mean that you're selfish

Having those boundary lines around you helps you take better care of yourself so that you're able to care for others. Remember, if your cup is empty, what will you share with others?

They don't have to be set in stone

Changing your boundaries from time to time won't make you look wishy-washy. On the contrary, it just means that you're open to change and growth. You're allowed to modify your boundaries if what you currently have doesn't work for you.

They won't hurt others or make them leave you

Make no mistake, a boundary is simply the way you tell someone that you deserve respect and the manner in which you'd like to be treated. Sure, it may be uncomfortable for some people, but that's not harmful. Also, people who see your boundaries as hurtful are indirectly indicating that they think you don't deserve the respect of being treated the way you'd prefer. Chew on that for a bit.

They won't make you become angry

Some people say that they've tried setting boundaries with some particular people in their lives and it just led to them getting angry a lot because those boundaries kept getting violated. Guess what? Even when you didn't have those clear-cut demarcations in place, you still got angry or resentful whenever your natural boundary was violated. Laid-down boundaries just makes it more obvious. As you keep asserting your boundaries over time, you'll find that you're getting less angry.

They don't have to look like anyone else's boundaries

It's tempting to want to emulate someone else's boundaries, especially if we greatly admire that person. However, boundaries don't look the same for everyone. It's more effective to set boundaries that apply specifically to your life and work best for you.

What other misconceptions do you have around setting boundaries? I would be delighted to hear about them via email. Now, let's break down these objections one by one, shall we?

How to Set Boundaries with Your Family

Setting boundaries with family members can be tricky, especially if your relationship with them is toxic in one way or another. However it's important for you to understand that your needs are valid. While you may not want to hurt the other person's feelings, you need to understand that they won't think twice about hurting yours. Yep. Repeatedly violating your boundaries really means that they can't be bothered about your feelings and they don't mind walking all over you for their own benefit.

Be clear and direct

This isn't the time to quibble. Tell your family what your needs are, and attach consequences if they violate your boundaries.

Be realistic

Just because you've summoned the courage to set out your boundaries, doesn't mean that your toxic family members will suddenly play nice. Understanding that maintaining your boundaries is where the work lies is the key to setting great boundaries.

Show them that your time is precious

Wasting time is an unfortunate result of poor boundary setting, and preventing this is crucial, as it's a great way to halt meaningless activities. Simply state that you need to attend to something else that's important or that your time is running out. You can point out that they're eating into your precious time as you make your excuses to leave.

Spend more time with people who appreciate you

There's a stark difference between people who don't respect you and people who actually value you. In the company of the latter, you're more likely to be relaxed, content, and happy. You may learn to see yourself in a different way than you're used to. When you spend more time with people that love and respect you, you're reminded that your feelings do count and you're not likely to accept anything less.

Tactics for Setting Boundaries and Maintaining Friendships

After proper evaluation, especially in light of the new information you now possess, you may find that you need to modify your relationships with your friends. Setting boundaries in this case can be hard; finding the balance such that your friendship isn't adversely affected can be a difficult balancing act. The fact remains, however, that our friends are such a huge part of our lives that the effect of a properly constructed boundary to protect that relationship with them is immediately felt.

You may need to check the boundaries of the relationship if you feel like you're the one doing all the work, you don't trust their integrity, you don't find their teasing funny, they don't respect your time, or maybe you're simply not as available as you used to be. Once you're dissatisfied with any area of the friendship, it's time to speak up.

A few things to keep in mind when setting boundaries for a friendship are:

Emphasize how valuable the friendship is to you

Explain that you're doing this to protect this important relationship. Truthfully, setting boundaries can be hurtful in this kind of scenario, but it's for the best. Explain that you're having this difficult conversation precisely because you care.

Be kind, firm, and direct

Let me say this now: setting a weak boundary is worse than not setting one in the first place because you'll spend valuable time and effort trying to reinforce it. It's better to steel yourself to set a strong boundary once and for all. This will reduce the likelihood of being frustrated or disappointed later on.

Start as soon as possible

If you've noticed a particular behavior that you don't like, set a boundary to deal with it as soon as possible so that it doesn't become a habit. It's also better to handle it quickly before it becomes a huge issue.

Don't focus on them

Using statements that start with "I" is a much more effective way to have the conversation. This way, your friend won't feel like you're blaming them, and you're centering the discussion on how you feel. It helps them to better understand where you're coming from and meet you halfway.

How to Create Boundaries in the Workplace for a More Positive Working Environment

Setting boundaries at work is more than just putting that nosy coworker in their place. It encompasses more than standing up to your toxic boss once and for all. Yeah, it's a whole lot more than that. It's realizing that you need to take care of yourself in the best way possible so that you can be as productive as possible in your career.

Setting boundaries at work utilizes the same basic idea as setting them anywhere else, but most people seem to discard thoughts of their wellbeing at work when they get caught up in the corporate hustle and bustle. If that's you, this is your sign to stop today.

So ask yourself: "What are the factors I need to have in place to be my most productive self?" Proper consideration will reveal that this question is the basis of every effective boundary you'll need to set because it encompasses your micromanaging, toxic manager as well as your nosy coworker.

Here are a few other tips to help you along the way:

Ask for help

If you have a supportive manager or a coworker who seems to be more productive, it won't hurt to ask them for some assistance. Apart from making you more effective, it also improves your relationship with them and may even blossom into a mentorship.

Decide your own limits

Now that you have an idea of your most productive environment, it's time to create it. If that means taking paid time off every quarter or insisting that you shouldn't be contacted after hours, then by all means make those decisions.

Communicate clearly to your team members and superiors

Once you have decided your limits, the next step is to communicate them to your team members. It's important to be as clear and direct as possible. Don't waffle about your boundaries, either; if you don't want to be reachable while on vacation, insist on it.

Get ready for the blowback

Did you think it was going to be that easy? I hope you didn't. You need to prepare for the consequences of your boundaries. This is where the toxic people at work start creeping out of the woodwork to make these boundaries difficult to maintain. But you won't be bothered because you already know that maintaining your boundaries takes a larger chunk of effort than setting them and you're appropriately prepared to stand by them, right? Great.

Setting Boundaries with Your Partner

This may be the aspect of setting boundaries that makes you the most uncomfortable. If you have a codependent partner with narcissistic traits, this may not be a walk in the park for you.

I'll say this right off the bat: putting up boundaries in that kind of relationship won't be pleasant, and your toxic partner won't take it lightly either. I think it's best that you're aware of this because, like they say, to be forewarned is to be forearmed.

Now, I know setting boundaries with a romantic partner feels like you're putting up walls between each other when you should be letting down your hair and being as vulnerable as possible. Yeah, it seems weird and counterintuitive, but trust me, that's not the case at all.

Even in a romantic relationship, you need to protect yourself and your values so that you can bring forth the best version of yourself. It's as simple as that. Yeah, you may be tempted to just keep holding on in the face of abuse and disrespect, but that's only harming you mentally and emotionally. You don't deserve that.

Your boundaries should reflect your important values and needs. This can look like:

- Asking for space to process emotionally weighty issues or to just breathe.
- Maintaining your identity outside your relationship by preserving your passions, interests, and hobbies.

- Separating your feelings from your partner's feelings. Don't let them assume your feelings or reactions.

- Saying no. If you truly feel uncomfortable with something, it's best to say no with the knowledge that you're preserving your relationship.

- Resisting emotional manipulation. Instead of taking the easy way out by accepting the blame even when you're not at fault, stick up for yourself.

- Asking to be respected. You deserve to have your opinions, emotions, and words respected, so don't hesitate to ask for it.

- Defending yourself when your partner tries to belittle you. Quickly speak up for yourself, state what you don't like, and ask for an apology.

- Deciding whether or not to be vulnerable with your partner. You should only open up when you feel safe, not because of pressure.

The bottom line is that realizing that intimate relationships need boundaries even more than non-intimate relationships will guide you when it comes to finding the willpower needed to reinforce your boundaries.

Imagine a situation where you're barely communicating with your partner because you're too full of resentment and frustration. Imagine constantly being unhappy but unable to communicate it for fear of hurting their feelings. If you're truly in a loving and healthy relationship, your partner will feel awful once they realize that you've been unhappy and didn't tell them.

The most important person in this relationship is *you*. This means that you have to put your wellbeing first so that you can love and receive love the right way.

How to Express Your Boundaries and Avoid Arguments

I once worked with a young man who was so anxious about being confronted that he tolerated a lot of bad behavior from his friends, who were quite mean. We decided that he needed to work on his boundaries and assert his feelings. He was so terrified, but he came to see the necessity of that action. To make the process easier for him, before he confronted anyone, he'd walk away first and close his eyes while rehearsing how he'd set or reinforce his boundaries. It was a bit embarrassing for him, but he learned to get used to it, and in no time, he was standing up for himself without flinching.

—Stephen

We've talked a lot about setting boundaries, but you and I both know that it's not easy, especially if you hate confrontation. Well, you're in luck because I have a few strategies that'll help you set your boundaries without the fear of ruffling too many feathers:

1. Find out why you're so afraid of confrontation in the first place

The fact that you'd rather count the grains of sand in the Sahara than face conflict is a sign that you've internalized the notion that conflict isn't compatible with healthy or peaceful relationships. It most likely indicates some trauma that remains unresolved for you.

But if you take the time to understand that conflict can be healthy and even make the relationship better, then you have a stronger chance of setting and maintaining your boundaries without fear. This means exposing yourself to conflicting situations and allowing yourself to experience the emotions while evaluating them. Keeping a journal and/or meditating will come in handy here.

2. Do it early

Here's the naked truth: holding off on correcting someone or setting your boundary immediately only exposes you to similar incidents. You'll be increasingly irritated by their actions, and eventually you'll explode because you just can't take it anymore. Trust me, that day will be messy and complicated and may end up damaging a precious friendship or relationship. Why wait till then? If you speak out now, you're likely to be calm and rational with a higher chance of avoiding more conflict further down the road.

3. Mind your language

Yep, something as simple as the way you present your thoughts can be pivotal in avoiding confrontation. Ensure that you place a lot of emphasis on the fact that you're not opposing the other person and that you appreciate and value their needs too.

Help them understand that you want the relationship to last a long time, in a healthy environment, and that's why you're speaking out. Focus more on how you feel rather than accusing them.

I don't know about you, but these tactics have helped me salvage a lot of relationships, and I'm happier for it. I'm grateful to have these techniques in my toolbelt. I'm sure you will be too!

How to Handle People Who Violate Your Boundaries

Okay, we both know that your boundaries are going to be tested by people around you, just to see how serious you are. If you stand your ground, some people will adjust and respect them. Unfortunately, others (read: the toxic narcs and codependents in your life) will violently oppose them. I don't mean to sound negative, but they will.

These people will ignore you and your demands and even get defensive when you challenge them. That's not all, folks—these people are horrible at reaching a compromise and may even try to persuade you to relax your boundaries. Oh, did I say "persuade"? My bad, I meant *manipulate*.

Here are a few helpful ways to handle those situations when they arise:

Recheck your boundaries

Before you storm off to accuse someone of violating your boundary, do a thorough evaluation. Did you set clear, consistent boundaries? Or did you keep changing the terms at every interaction with the person? Has the person seen you enforcing that boundary with others? You also need to be crystal clear about the boundary in your own mind and stick to it; that way you won't be tempted to adjust it. If you do an assessment and you're certain that your boundaries are clear and consistent, then you can move on to the next step. If not, you need to redefine them and make sure you're enforcing them consistently.

Reassert your boundaries

Yeah, I know. It's most likely an exercise in futility to reiterate a boundary when it's already been violated, but it's necessary to stay consistent even when you can't control the outcome. This is the perfect time to state the consequences that come with violating the boundary and enact them. For example:

"If you don't stop yelling at me, I'm going to hang up."

Or,

"If you keep talking over me, I'm going to end this conversation and leave the room."

Then, you should hang up or leave the room or do whatever consequence is attached to that boundary violation.

Face the facts

Look, as much as you don't want to hear it, it's necessary to realize that some people will never accept your boundaries. Narcissists are very competitive and will not give in easily. In such cases, it may be easier to limit contact or reframe the context of the relationship.

I need to say that this isn't the same thing as giving up because the average narc will never let you win fair and square. In fact, I'd say that it's simply about you seeing the writing on the wall and protecting yourself. This way you're not available for them to manipulate and control. Sounds like a win to me.

Your Quick Workbook: Healthy Boundaries Worksheet

1. Identify the toxic behavior: Write down specific examples of the toxic behavior that you want to address.

_____

_____

_____

_____

2. Assess the impact: How does the person's toxic behavior affect you emotionally, physically, mentally, and spiritually?

_____

_____

_____

_____

3. Define your boundaries: What are the specific behaviors and actions that you will not tolerate from the toxic person?

_____

_____

_____

_____

_____

4. Communicate your boundaries: Clearly communicate your boundaries to the toxic person in a calm, assertive manner. Be specific and avoid making accusations or attacking the person. Write down how you're going to express your boundaries to this person.

_____

_____

_____

_____

5. Enforce your boundaries: If the toxic person continues with the same behavior, it is important to enforce your boundaries by taking concrete steps. Write down what step you're going to take for this particular person.

_____

_____

_____

_____

6. Review and reassess: Regularly evaluate the situation and reassess your boundaries to ensure they are still aligned with your needs and values. It's your first time setting boundaries with this person; as time goes on, things might change that cause you to review your boundaries. Also, how often do you think this assessment should be done?

_____

_____

_____

_____

Remember, setting healthy boundaries with toxic people is an ongoing process, and it's important to be kind and compassionate to yourself during this time.

Chapter Six Takeaway

Creating boundaries is crucial to your wellbeing, but it must be done with the right mindset. If you create boundaries with the mindset of keeping people away from you, then you'll quickly realize that those boundaries become walls that lock you in and prevent you from any meaningful interactions with others.

PART TWO

Emotional Abuse Recovery

One possible scenario in dealing with narcissists is being bound together with one in a legal union, like marriage. If you're in such a situation, you might be wondering, "What do I do?" That's one of the questions this final part of this book attempts to answer.

In the pages ahead, I will guide you through how to handle narcissistic relationships without losing your mind. However, in the event that you can no longer manage such a relationship, this part will also guide you on how to transition into a new life where you'll enjoy much tranquility.

You won't want to miss the climax of this book. The next two chapters comprise the point where you'll learn to untangle, detoxify, and heal completely. The secret to your best life yet is waiting to be discovered in this final part.

Turn to the next page, and the next after it, till your thirst is quenched.

So far, if you've discovered something meaningful in reading this book, please click here to leave a review on Amazon. That will help other people in their personal growth.

What to Do When You Can't Leave: Communicating with a Toxic Person

BY SETTING BOUNDARIES

"A word fitly spoken is like apples of gold in settings of silver."

—Proverbs 25:11

"I used to think the worst thing in life was to end up all alone. It's not. The worst thing in life is ending up with people who make you feel all alone."

—Robin Williams

There's a class of people that is difficult to love: toxic people. With this kind of person, there's no special season that has them emitting some inner beauty. They constantly exude an aura of toxicity. It's who they are. These people might be physically beautiful, but their attitudes are draining and exhausting. The aura they carry makes it difficult to deal with them or even have meaningful conversations without experiencing pain.

I hope and pray you meet someone ready to do life with you without seeing you as an antagonist. I hope you have relationships that add value to you.

The truth is that we don't recognize toxic folks at the beginning. They may have become part of our lives, and there's little we can do to keep them at bay. They could be an estranged spouse or a baby mama or baby daddy. If children are involved, you might be sentenced to a long time of having to communicate with them. It's even worse if that person is a narcissist. It's no news that narcissists are difficult people. Not just that, they're hard to reason with. With a child in the equation, you're stuck with the narcissist, especially if they're bent on being in the child(ren)'s life.

Why Narcissists Are Hard to Reason With

If you've ever stuttered or lashed out in frustration while conversing with someone, you'll relate to the fact that some folks are hard to reason with. Have you ever gotten to a point where you nodded your head in frustration, then paused in the middle of a conversation like a laborer taking a break from trying to cut down a huge tree? Have you ever felt parts of your body tremble after a conversation? Do you find yourself crying after interacting with a particular person? Do you experience a sporadic change in your mood after speaking with this person?

These are just some of the things you'll experience when you're trying to reason with a toxic person. It's even worse when the individual is a narcissist. The question now is, why are they so hard to deal with? Why are they bent on being contrary, even if what you're saying is reasonable? The answer isn't difficult to decipher. It's engraved in their personality, so much so that they don't think they have a problem. That makes it even worse. You can't ostracize them from who they are.

Without further ado, let's dive right into it. Here are some of the reasons you can't seem to agree with that narcissist in your life.

Entitlement

When it comes to narcissism, entitlement can be defined as feeling like you deserve to get certain benefits regardless of whether you earned them or not. People can feel entitled to your money, gifts, time, attention, or any other thing that could be perceived to be of value. When the word "entitlement" pops up in a conversation, it's often accompanied by signs of disgust—but I want you to know that entitlement can be both good and bad.

Entitlement simply means that you have a right to access certain privileges as a member of a particular space based on your membership or contributions. It can be good in the sense that you're aware of your rights as an individual within your sphere of influence, whether it's in the aspect of class, race, creed, socio-economic status, or a system. Entitlement can be specific to a particular relationship, situation, or place.

In a home, a child is entitled to proper care and nurturing from their parent irrespective of the child's behavior because he/she was brought into the world by the parent. As a citizen of a country, you believe that you're entitled to social amenities and other government benefits because you pay taxes. Even as humans, we are entitled to love, respect, and honor irrespective of age, class, or social standing. Don't all the religions of the world agree on this one view—loving our neighbor? Isn't that a command from God most of humanity believes in? The examples I have listed are healthy forms of entitlement.

However, narcissists represent a different type of entitlement. This is one central feature of narcissism that makes communication difficult. Entitlement manifests differently for grandiose and vulnerable narcissists. Since narcissists are self-absorbed people who are preoccupied with their own needs and feelings, they can't see the larger picture that involves others.

For grandiose narcissists, it's about getting the best of something without consideration for others. Usually, they want preferential treatment or consideration. For example, they might want to be attended to when they're paying for a public service even if it's not their turn. In the workplace, they might evade certain duties and responsibilities. At home, they might make emotional or financial demands without considering your needs. Everything is about them. It gets even more difficult when you're trying to communicate your needs.

For vulnerable narcissists, it's about wanting to be admired for their specialness and accomplishments. If they don't get this from people, they see it as a failure on their part or an implication that nobody likes them and that the world is against them. Consequently, they begin to play the victim and use it to justify their entitled behavior.

When a person believes he or she is being victimized when that isn't the case, how do you get through to them?

When a person believes he or she deserves to be served first in a restaurant, how do you communicate with them?

When a grown adult feels they must have their bills paid by a family member or friend, how do you make them see that the world doesn't revolve around them?

This is why setting boundaries is important when it comes to narcissists. Very important.

Lack of Empathy

It's difficult to communicate easily with someone who doesn't feel what you feel. Is that not what empathy is all about? Isn't it about putting oneself in another's shoes? Isn't it about imagining what it's like to experience what another person is experiencing and seeing things from their point of view? Narcissists are incapable of feeling what you feel because they're so consumed with their own needs. A person that's devoid of empathy acts cold and insensitive even in the face of intense emotion. It's like bullets bouncing off a bulletproof vest. When you're trying to converse with a narcissist, they are most likely going to dismiss your feelings.

Due to inattention and self-focus, narcissists will not feel what you feel, they won't see what you see, and they most definitely won't think what you think. Hence, communication fails before it even begins.

Exploitation

The language of exploitation does not include reason, logic, or morals in its lexicon. Exploitation is about using others to gratify your own desires. In our narcissistically-blossoming world, you can see governments exploiting workers, corporations exploiting rural communities, partners exploiting one another in relationships, and bosses exploiting subordinates. The list is endless. In a relationship, exploitation can be financial, physical, or emotional, and it's about having an advantage over the other person.

Sometimes exploitation feeds on ignorance, and sometimes it's unintentional. If a person or group doesn't realize they are being exploited, it won't stop.

The goal is to have an advantage, to dominate and control. Trying to confront or communicate your needs to someone bent on being in control is like hitting a brick wall. You won't easily have conversations with a narcissist when they're all about forcing people into putting them on a pedestal and showing gratuitous displays of respect.

In some other subtle forms of exploitative abuse of power, narcissistic parents can shove unfulfilled dreams, goals, or fantasies down a child's throat just to feel good about themselves. It can also come in the form of forcing children to imbibe the parent's thoughts or behavior, rather than allowing them to develop their own ideas and interests.

It's hard to communicate with narcissists when they're so focused on controlling you. Oftentimes, they sincerely think they're doing you a lot of good. Other times, they're comfortable with you being under their control. It's an affront to their ego and grandiosity that you have a mind of your own. Think of how exhausting it could be to try to get someone like that to see things from your angle.

How to Communicate with a Toxic Person and Still Keep Your Sanity

My relationship with a covert narcissist taught me that communication is work. Actually, it's not just work—it's an art. It's something that has to be studied and understood amid a world that's saturated with so much information and yet devoid of wisdom. In a world where everyone has something to say, it takes a lot of guts to listen. It takes discipline.

In the words of Earl Wilson, "Listening, not imitation, may be the sincerest form of flattery." Winston Churchill's views align with Wilson's, as he once said, "Courage is what it takes to stand up and speak; courage is also what it takes to sit down and listen." As sincere and true as these words are, it's something that toxic people resent. They'd rather have you roll in the mud with them than stare at them as if they were an actor on stage. When it comes to communicating with toxic people, you must know what to say and what not to say.

Now, let me tell you something. You'll learn to say the right thing if you know how to listen. In today's narcissistic world, folks only listen to give a clapback. The goal is not usually to understand but to give a piece of their minds. This is why there's chaos, leading to a break in communication. Let your goals be to understand, and then be understood.

Learn to listen

This is not just about listening. It's about active listening. This is about having clarity about what the other person is trying to say. By the time you're clear about the other person's views, you're capable of dealing with them healthily and more effectively.

Active listening is different from just listening. With the former, you're listening to understand what the person is saying and where they're coming from with all their claims and outbursts. It's difficult to listen when the speaker's comments are getting under your skin, but when you come to an understanding that it's not about you but about what they might be battling within themselves, you'll listen more.

Make sure your body language and tone aren't aggravating the situation

Without knowing it, you might be displaying body language that is quite confrontational. Even if you're silent, is your body language screaming for a fight? Your body language might be trivializing or challenging what the other person is saying.

For example, are you saying "I'm sorry," but your tone sounds nonchalant? Is your nonchalance accompanied with arms folded across your chest defiantly?

Sometimes, an "I'm sorry" is exactly what a toxic person *doesn't* want to hear.

I don't mean that you should apologize because you're in the wrong, but at times, you'll need to be brave enough to lay aside your pride to allow for your peace of mind and to avoid dragging the issue out. Try saying something like, "I'm sorry you feel this way."

Don't get drawn in. Just remain calm.

Limit time spent together

Time spent with a toxic individual can be draining. If you find yourself feeling drained and stressed after spending time with someone, you might have to keep your distance. When every conversation leads to a fight and a repetitive violation of boundaries, it's high time you took a step backwards and reduced your communication with such folks.

Set boundaries

Being aware of yourself and understanding what ticks you off and prevents you from becoming a better person is one major step towards setting boundaries, especially with toxic individuals. Let folks know what you like and what you dislike. You can adjust the dynamics of your relationship with toxic people based on your boundaries.

Walk away

Did you know that some people have wound up in jail because they didn't walk away from a toxic confrontation? Because they got triggered, they moved from being the victim to being the villain. To avoid this, plan an exit strategy by saying something like, "I'm sorry, I have to leave now. I don't like where this conversation is headed," or, "I suggest we talk when you're calm." Then take a walk.

Don't look at this list as another set of rules. These are necessary steps for keeping a clear mind when communicating with toxic individuals. The toxicity of an individual is never about you. As someone once said, "The goodness in you irritates their demons." Don't lose your sanity, but rather guard it jealously.

Expressing Your Needs and Truth in Every Relationship

When it comes to those we love, we make excuses for them. We make compromises for them. We hardly hold them to the standards that we would other people.

Talk about the things we do for love! In our fear of losing them, we let go of our own needs. Sometimes we let go of ourselves. We let go of our Truth and relish in the lie we tell ourselves. If care is not taken, you might end up seeing your mistreatment as a sign of love.

It's high time you started having difficult conversations. If you don't address the issues in your relationships, you will end up harboring resentment, overthinking, and experiencing irritation and anxiety. Issues that are always swept under the carpet will lead to a mountain of conflicts in the long run if communication is absent.

For any relationship to thrive, openness is important. How do you begin?

Know what you want

You must be aware of your needs. Do you know that at times you get moody and sad without being able to place a finger on the reason? Many times we can only get answers when we do a soul search into what might be missing. It's hidden somewhere in your subconscious. To help keep track of your thoughts, you can write them down. After a while, you'll find the answers. Take time out to figure out what's bothering you. It might be a need for connection, communication, emotional intimacy, physical intimacy, independence, or other needs that are not being met.

Arrange a rendezvous

Make preparations to meet at a time and place that's comfortable for you both. Make sure it's a quiet and serene place that will help you focus on your conversation. It's best to have this conversation when your partner is well-rested and energized, ready to listen to anything you have to say.

Don't be accusatory

Now that you're ready to bare your mind, don't begin your statements with comments like, "You never…" or "You're always…" Statements like this will put your partner on the defensive and can lead to an argument. Instead, say, "I feel like…"

You can begin by stating the good qualities of your relationship before moving to the problem. Make it all about you. Don't direct it towards your partner. It should be about you talking about your experiences and how you feel about them without making your partner look like the bad guy in the picture.

Avoid blaming or complaining. Don't say things like, "I need you to…" That's accusatory and can lead to another wave of arguments. When you make your conversations less accusatory, you make it a situation of "us against the problem."

DO'S DONT'S WORKSHEET

FAMILY MEMBERS

DO'S	DONT'S
Visiting during holidays	Visiting unannounced

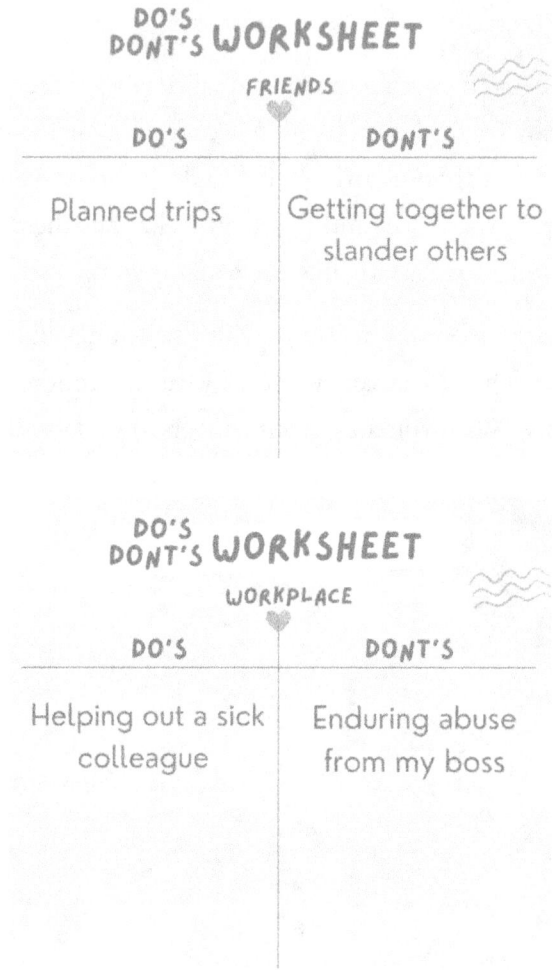

**DO'S
DONT'S WORKSHEET**

FRIENDS

DO'S	DONT'S
Planned trips	Getting together to slander others

**DO'S
DONT'S WORKSHEET**

WORKPLACE

DO'S	DONT'S
Helping out a sick colleague	Enduring abuse from my boss

Figuring Out When You Should and Shouldn't be Sorry

"I'm sorry" is one of the most abused and trivialized statements ever made. Nonetheless, it's still one of the most difficult to say. Many have made it such a habit that it has lost its soothing effect on the hurting. Many a time, it's an indication that a person hasn't learned their lesson.

Apologizing is a skill. You have to know how best to go about it. Sometimes "I'm sorry" doesn't suffice for the gravity of the offense. On the other hand, due to the manipulative nature of some people in our lives, we tend to get guilt-tripped for choosing what's best for us because it doesn't sit well with them, and we end up apologizing for things for which we shouldn't be sorry. For others, it might be the way we were raised, and apologizing has become instinctive.

These are times when you *should* be sorry:

1. When you use derogatory remarks towards your partner in a fit of anger

2. When you start an argument

3. When you're nonchalant about the relationship

4. When you're emotionally and physically unavailable when your partner needs you

5. When you forget special events or occasions that mean a lot to your partner

6. When you refuse to pay heed to the yearnings of your partner

7. When you're harsh, rude, or sarcastic about critical matters

8. When you cross a boundary that has already been clearly stated

Now, these are things that you *shouldn't* be sorry for:

1. Don't be sorry for calling out a person for their bad attitude and behavior.

2. Don't be sorry for setting boundaries.

3. Don't be sorry for stating your needs.

4. Don't be sorry for saying no.

5. Don't be sorry for being assertive.

6. Don't be sorry for standing up for yourself.

7. Don't be sorry for expressing your displeasure about a wrong done to you.

8. Don't be sorry for speaking the truth when the need arises.

We must be clear on the things we should be sorry for and those we shouldn't. When we're clear about this disparity, we are less susceptible to manipulation from toxic individuals.

Saying No Without Feeling Guilty

People-pleasing is common amongst those who have frequently been made to feel guilty for saying no. This class of people easily fall prey to toxic manipulators who are ready to manipulate your vulnerabilities and insecurities.

Remember:

- You can say no without feeling bad about it.
- You can say no without feeling like a villain or standoffish person.
- Sometimes you have to say no for your convenience.
- Sometimes you have to say no to protect yourself.
- Sometimes you have to say no to set boundaries.

Some people don't say no effectively. Instead, they make excuses. This leaves room for more requests from the person making a request. There are several ways that you can say no effectively.

1. Say, "No." Yup! Just say it. There's no point beating around the bush and making excuses. If you have to explain, do so briefly. But never feel compelled or coerced into doing something that you aren't keen on doing.

2. Be assertive about your decision. You don't have to be rude about it. You gain control over the situation when you say things like, "I'm sorry, I won't be able to do that right now, but if I can, I'll let you know." While

saying no, let your body language also say no. Don't give an air of not being sure about your decision.

3. Boundaries must be set. If you're in a relationship with someone, you might have issues saying no to them. Saying no allows people to understand your stance on certain issues. Knowing yourself and the dynamics of your relationship will make it easier to say no.

Your Quick Workbook

Here is a simple worksheet to help you communicate with toxic people in your life:

1. Identify the toxic behavior: What specifically is the toxic behavior you are trying to address?

_____

_____

_____

_____

2. Reflect on your feelings: Take some time to think about how the toxic behavior makes you feel and how it affects your relationship with the person.

_____

_____

_____

_____

3. Set clear boundaries: What are the boundaries you need to set in order to protect yourself?

_____

_____

_____

_____

4. Choose a calm time and place: When and where will you have the conversation? Choose a time and place where you both can be calm and won't be interrupted.

_____

_____

_____

_____

5. Stay focused on the behavior, not the person: Remember to focus on the behavior you want to change, not attacking the person themselves. It's easy to get angry in this situation, which is why you should remind yourself of the behavior here:

_____

_____

_____

_____

6. Use "I" statements: Express your feelings and needs using "I" statements, such as "I feel hurt when you do/say x." Let's practice—write down what you'll say:

_____

_____

_____

7. Listen to their perspective: Try to understand the other person's point of view and let them know you are open to hearing their thoughts.

8. Find common ground: What areas do you think you both agree on? Where can you work together to resolve the issue?

9. Agree on a solution: Work together to find a solution that works for both of you.

10. Follow up: Check in to make sure the solution is working and to hold both parties accountable.

Remember, effective communication with toxic people requires patience, empathy, and a strong sense of self. The goal is to find a solution that works for both of you and to maintain healthy boundaries for yourself.

Chapter Seven Takeaway

Having to stay in contact with a narcissist can be hard. But it is in times like this I want you to remember something: you're in control of yourself, not the other person. The narcissist can behave how he or she wants to behave, but you're the one with the final say on your response.

Loving and Prioritizing Yourself When Dealing with Narcissists

"For no one ever hated his own flesh, but nourishes and cherishes it, just as Christ does the church."

—Ephesians 5:29, ESV

"The challenge is not to be perfect—it is to be whole."

—Jane Fonda

Overcoming Narcissistic Victim Syndrome for Good

People react to narcissists in different ways. Your reception to a narcissist can be attributed to your exposure to narcissistic behavior, especially in your formative years.

If you were nurtured by narcissistic parents, constantly teased or scorned by your siblings, or were a timid child that got abused or exploited, your trust has been violated repeatedly. This will make you more paranoid and sensitive than others who don't share your experiences.

From our knowledge of social history, we know that we have expectations of other people and we feel about the people around us. This explains why the most important step in dealing with narcissists is studying the patterns that make up our experiences and how our reactions bring pain to us. For example, your tendency to people-please has likely exposed you to the whim and caprices of the narcissist. Maybe your lack of boundaries has made narcissists trample on your self-esteem.

The moment you begin to see the role that you've played in your own pain, you'll begin to be able to impede the cycle of pain that we allow narcissists to inflict on us.

I know it's easier said than done. You're probably screaming, "It's not that simple!"

Yes, I know.

Narcissists aren't always negative. We see them as this larger-than-life entity and then put them on a pedestal. We can't imagine our lives without them. We surrender to an illusion and end up losing ourselves, getting bruised and feeling empty.

Here's how you can rid yourself of narcissistic victim syndrome for good:

1. Pay attention to how you're feeling. I remember someone telling me, "Energy doesn't lie." I've held on to that. If you're constantly feeling uneasiness, anger, shame, and fear while in the company of a particular person, this can be a telltale sign that you're in the presence of a narcissist. The moment you sense this, it's best to take a step back and seek ways to defend yourself.

2. Once you identify these feelings, pay attention to what buttons are being pushed to trigger you. This is why self-awareness is important. This way, you know when a narcissist is trying to hit a nerve. You know you've felt this same way in the past. Do a soul search and own your narcissistic vulnerabilities. Are you easily shamed by condescending comments? Do you feel so low that you're bent on pleasing people even to your detriment? These are questions that you need to ask yourself.

3. Now that you've identified your weaknesses, which the narcissist recognizes, move to your feelings. How have your feelings enabled narcissists in their devices?

4. Separate yourself from any form of self-loathing that the narcissist might evoke in you. Recognize that their projections do not define you. It's a form of control to keep them dominating. It'll help you to see them in a less-grandiose light when you realize that they put you down to feel superior. The more you give them admiration, the more you feed their narcissistic supply.

5. After detaching yourself from this self-loathing, resist the urge to retaliate. Don't stoop to their level. Keep in mind that it's baseless to challenge them or preach to them about the error of their ways. Save yourself the effort and walk away. Narcissists are comfortable in their delusions, so much so that the truth about themselves lies dormant in their subconscious. And you know what? They want to keep it that way.

What am I saying? Don't waste your breath trying to resurrect a truth that they choose to leave in the subconscious. It can only worsen matters. Don't even think about it.

Detoxifying After Years of Emotional Abuse

You must have heard a lot about detoxification in the world of physical wellness. Your mind, which determines the course of your life, also needs detoxifying. This isn't about detoxing your mind from negative emotions. This isn't about ending suffering. It's more about being in touch with your feelings, understanding the roots of those feelings, coming to terms with your pain, and not allowing it to distract you from truly living.

It's about clearing out the residue of wrong mindsets and emotions that remain engraved in your subconscious. Did you know that your trauma still lurks around in your mind? Could that be the reason you're experiencing constant mood swings? Could that be the reason you still have PTSD from an experience that changed your life?

Do you know why the mind has to come first when it comes to healing from emotional abuse?

Psychiatrist Bessel Van Der Kolk, MD (author of *The Body Keeps the Score: Brain, Mind, and Body in the Healing of Trauma*) states, "Research revealed that trauma produces actual physiological changes, including recalibration of the brain's alarm system, an increase in stress hormone activity, and alterations in the system that filters relevant information from irrelevant" (2014). So, the state of your emotions is connected to how your body functions effectively.

Let's look at these emotional toxins and their roots.

- Hurt is rooted in victimization, helplessness and blame.
- Sadness is rooted in self-pity and regret.

- Shame is rooted in humiliation and embarrassment.

- Hopelessness is rooted in loneliness, despair, and desperation.

- Fear is rooted in anxiety, panic, and immobilization.

- Anger is rooted in resentment and bitterness.

- Hate is rooted in meanness and vengefulness.

- Jealousy is rooted in insecurities, envy, and possessiveness.

- Pride is rooted in self-righteousness and self-exaltation.

- Greed is rooted in insatiability and emotional hunger.

- Guilt is rooted in unhealthy responsibility and self-blame.

- Criticism is rooted in judgment and false projections.

How can you detox yourself emotionally? How do you go about a soul purge? Let's dive into some useful techniques.

1. Identify your triggers and their roots. Once you're aware of these things, you can seek self-soothing ways to take charge of your emotions. You can try relaxation rituals to help you relax, like meditation, prayer, laughter, or listening to classical music (or some other genre of music that keeps you calm).

2. Now that you're aware of what triggers you, plan out how you can keep yourself in check when the need

arises. If you've got anger issues, plan to go on a walk in the moment. Don't say a word. Don't pick up anything. Just take that walk. If someone is trying to put you down, separate yourself from what's been said. Understand that what's been said is an expression of the other person's insecurities. It has nothing to do with you. You're good.

3. Take up a charitable course. It's high time you started living. To do this, you'll need to step outside yourself. The more absorbed you are with your emotional instability, the more you'll miss out on how much good you can do for the world around you. Have you considered mentoring young people, volunteering, checking up on a sick friend, or even simply listening to another's problem? You'll see how much healing will come from just breathing life into the things and people around you.

4. Take a break from complaining. There's surely something to be grateful for. This isn't trivializing your emotional challenges or ignoring that something is wrong; rather, it's accepting that some things can be overwhelming, but that you can quit complaining and be grateful for the seemingly inconsequential things that you rarely pay attention to. The moment you cease

complaining, positive thoughts will begin to flood your mind.

5. Know your vices. Are you fond of binge eating or reaching for the bottle when you're in distress? Tell yourself the truth about what's making you over-indulge. These emotional vices that are causing you anxiety might just be rooted in something you're afraid to confront. When you identify them, it will be much easier to limit and control your addictions to these vices.

6. Get help. When I say help, I don't mean your friend, family, or next-door neighbor. I'm not saying they aren't helpful in soothing your pain—you need them— but you need a professional too. With therapy, you'll exhume all that trauma, the buried emotions and anxieties that are holding you back from being your best self. You don't have to be going through a meltdown to go to therapy. Look at this as a luxurious treat that you choose to give your mind.

7. Take on a 7-Day Challenge with God. Sit down in a silent place and spend 30 minutes meditating on His Word for 7 days.

Think of the furnishing of your mind when it comes to emotional detox. Your body and organs will thank you for it.

Don't Blame Yourself

The older you get, the more you'll realize that there are some things that you shouldn't blame yourself for. After exiting a relationship, it's not uncommon for people to blame themselves for the pain they went through. Before I get ahead of myself, let's dive into some of the things you shouldn't blame yourself for.

1. Don't blame yourself for being rejected. Oftentimes, we internalize rejection and make it all about ourselves when truly it's never about us. Find your tribe. You aren't for everyone, and that's okay.

2. Don't blame yourself for expressing your emotions. This is what makes you real. There's no such thing as "doing too much" when it comes to emotions. The sooner you accept this, the more you'll embrace your authentic self. (This applies as long as you're not inflicting physical harm or being emotionally abusive.)

3. Don't blame yourself for making mistakes. It's part of being human. Focus on being a better person today than you were yesterday. It's time to move forward.

4. Don't blame yourself for having needs. Others might treat your needs as if they don't matter. It doesn't mean that they don't.

5. Don't blame yourself for another's insecurities. Sometimes people try to treat you badly and project their insecurities onto you. It's not your fault.

6. Don't blame yourself for looking out for yourself. There's nothing wrong with taking care of yourself. Sometimes you need to, for you to be healthy for others.

7. Don't blame yourself for being too trusting. Humans are flawed. If we don't take risks when it comes to love, we're not truly living. Treat failed relationships as a lesson and an opportunity to grow and evolve.

8. Don't blame yourself for the pains of the past. The past is the past. The only direction you need to be looking is forward. Decide to live in the now and work towards a brighter future.

How to Prioritize Yourself Every Day

Have you been a people-pleaser in the past, where you gave so much of yourself? Have you gotten hurt in the process of trying to win a certain someone's heart, only for it to get broken? How can you be a blessing to your world when you put yourself in positions that leave you hurt?

Here are simple ways that you can look out for yourself daily without feeling guilty about it.

1. Set apart a time for deep reflection. Revamp your thoughts, set your goals, do a review of your life, practice gratitude, and breathe. I had to add "breathe" there because many times we hold our breath out of anxiety and fear. Breathe.

2. Eat healthily. Fruits, vegetables, and other whole foods are readily available in markets and stalls. It gets even better when you complement a good diet with the right supplements. Doing an overall health checkup will let you know which vitamins and minerals you're deficient in.

3. Take breaks. Hustle culture has taught you that if you sleep a certain number of hours per day, you must be lazy. You don't have to work by these rules. Know your limits when it comes to your health. If your body is telling you that it's time to lie down, listen to it. Don't hesitate to take a break if you have to. And remember, screen time isn't taking a break. If you're taking a break, it has to be rest for all your senses.

4. Manage your time well. Set deadlines for yourself. Work effectively and manage your work well.

5. Drink water. Yep! Good old H2O. You can't deny the many benefits of water. Your organs will be cleansed, your skin will be moisturized, your joints will be well lubricated. And yes, you'll exude confidence when

you're glowing differently. Water ain't old school. Treat yourself to a lot of it.

Support Systems and Support Groups

One of the greatest gifts that we'll ever have is the gift of people. A support system is a network of people, be it family, friends, or peers, that are available to walk us through tough times. Imagine not having any friends to call on while in a relationship with a narcissist. That's dangerous, if you ask me.

One of the ploys of toxic people is to isolate you from loved ones. Don't fall for that ploy. However, in situations where it seems that the people close to you might not believe you when you explain the abuse, it's best to reach out to a formal support group. A support group is made up of people who are going through the same things you are. They are willing to listen without judging you or blaming you for your wrong choices.

Here are the benefits of having a support system, whether in the form of family and friends or a formal support group:

1. They help you stay strong in the face of loss, stress, or setbacks. They will even help you find the humor in those moments.

2. They will help you see the things you don't see in yourself and your relationships. They will change your perception of things and challenge you to grow.

3. They can help distract you from your worries, keep you feeling secure, and bring out the best in you.

4. They will provide you with guidance, support, and advice when you're at a crossroads about certain issues.

If you have friends, family, and loved ones that do this, keep them close. Never sacrifice your friendships or family relationships on the altar of your romantic ones.

If you're wondering how to get a support system in place, here are some suggestions.

1. Start volunteering. Commit to it and you will feel a sense of belonging through being around people that are working towards the same goals.

2. Engage with neighbors and colleagues at work. The conversation doesn't have to be all about work. You can talk with your coworkers about various ideas, ideologies, or issues that affect the world.

3. Start a book club. You'll not only widen your mental horizon, you'll also have the opportunity to see things in different ways through the perspectives of others.

4. Be active in your local community. Being involved in the community and making contributions to its development will provide protection for you as well.

Emotional Detoxification Worksheet

Honestly answer the following questions:

1. What are your triggers? Is there an event in your past that causes you to become angry when something similar occurs?

2. What's toxic about your reactions to those triggers? Do you inflict emotional or physical harm on others when angry?

3. What do you hope to do instead of reacting in an unhealthy manner? List your ideas.

4. How can you regulate those emotions?

5. List the bad habits that you hope to remove from your life.

6. What are some of your toxic behaviors that led you to these bad habits?

7. What are your insecurities? List them.

8. What do you hope to do to address those insecurities?

9. List out the qualities you want your future self to possess.

10. Affirm those qualities as if you already had them.

Note that you can write your wishes and affirmations on sticky notes and post them just above your desk or on your bathroom mirror as reminders. When you constantly see these affirmations, your resolve to be a better person will be strengthened.

Radical Self-Love Worksheet

1. Ignore the negative comments said about you. Write out a list of things that you love about yourself.

_____

_____

_____

_____

2. Now that you've listed great things about yourself, write out how you intend to care for your entire being, whether it's physically or emotionally.

_____

_____

_____

_____

3. List out the things or the people you're grateful for.

_____

_____

_____

These are some self-care techniques that I don't want you to forget:

1. Don't talk down to yourself.

2. Feel free to express your needs.

3. Be assertive when you feel that your boundaries are being violated.

4. Don't feel obligated to apologize for expressing your displeasure about a wrong.

5. Nurture yourself like you would a flower. List the things that bring you peace.

6. Let the past remain in the past. Make peace with it.

7. Make your health and happiness a priority.

8. Keep reminding yourself of your uniqueness every day.

9. Open your heart to loving again.

Self-Reflection and Self-Compassion for Healing Worksheet

1. Find a quiet, comfortable place where you won't be disturbed.

2. Take a few deep breaths and try to relax.

3. Reflect on your experiences as a victim of narcissistic abuse and try to understand how they have affected you. Acknowledge and validate your feelings.

4. Treat yourself as you would treat a friend who is going through a similar situation. Speak to yourself with kindness and understanding. Offer yourself words of comfort and encouragement.

5. Repeat positive affirmations to yourself, such as, "I am worthy of love and respect," "I am strong and resilient," and "I am deserving of a happy and fulfilling life."

6. Take some time to focus on your strengths, accomplishments, and things that bring you joy. Try to remember that your experiences do not define you, and that you have the power to create a new narrative for yourself.

7. When you are ready, slowly open your eyes and return to your day, carrying the feelings of self-compassion and self-worth with you.

Repeat this exercise as often as needed, meditate on God's Word, and try to incorporate self-reflection and self-compassion into your daily routine.

Chapter Eight Takeaway

Leaving a toxic relationship is a lot of work, and you should applaud yourself for this. However, it is equally important for you to remind yourself of what you left and the fact that you need to heal. It's easy to blame yourself for the abuse you suffered, but there is no use in that. Rather, revel in your newfound wisdom and rely on your support systems to carry you through.

You've got this!

A Much-Needed Biblical Roundup

In my experience, many Christians feel really guilty about setting boundaries. They think that it's unbecoming to say no when they're asked to make a sacrifice that they don't want to make. Well, the truth is that letting people erode your boundaries because you think that makes you look good is not a healthy way to approach life. I'll give you two important principles from the Bible to back up my views.

1. God loves a cheerful giver. Note the word: **cheerful**.

2. Even if you give up your body to be burned at the stake, without love, you're **nothing**.

Now, let's example these two principles.

2 Corinthians 9:7

"Each one must give as he has decided in his heart, not reluctantly or under compulsion, for God loves a cheerful giver."

God considers cheerfulness a really important ingredient whenever you're giving something—your money, time, energy, resources, support, or whatever. Without cheerfulness (and trust me, cheerfulness is always absent if you're feeling forced), your gift isn't acceptable to God. When you have boundaries that are clearly set, you'll have communicated without mincing words the extent to which you're willing to go for anything or anyone at any given point in time. That's you programming cheerfulness into your giving, thereby making it acceptable to God. Get it?

On point 2:

1 Corinthians 13:3

"If I give everything I own to the poor and even go to the stake to be burned as a martyr, but I don't love, I've gotten nowhere."

It's crazy, but it's possible to let people walk all over you, take your stuff without permission, show up to your house unannounced, and even gobble up your dinner, and yet you don't love them. But it's all empty—again, unacceptable to God. Doing "good things" without love is completely pointless and, if we're honest with ourselves, is just a waste of resources. Without setting boundaries, you'll inevitably find yourself having to do things that you really don't want to do even if they're supposed to be "good."

Boundary setting will keep you where you want to be. A lack of boundaries will always force you out of God's will because then you'll find yourself doing things you don't want to do for people you don't even like, and that, in God's sight, is hypocrisy.

Finding Peace with Godly Boundaries

In this world of turmoil and highly dysfunctional relationships, many people hesitate to enforce boundaries because of the initial conflict it brings. I want you to know that setting boundaries will bring you peace of mind, but I'm not going to sit here and tell you the big fat lie that you'll find that peace right away. At first, it'll most likely be full of struggles. The person you're settling boundaries against will revolt and might even resent you for a bit. Two things I want you to take note of here are:

1. Never, *never, ever* give up on your boundaries.

2. Give it time.

Even for the person setting boundaries, it can be a real tough one if you have mostly allowed people to get away with walking all over you in the past. Know for sure that this time, though it may not be easy at first, your boundaries will work as long as you stick with them.

Above all, pray for strength to go through with this and let the joy of the Lord energize you.

Here are a few Scriptures to help you find peace as you carry on with this journey:

"The Lord gives strength to his people, and the Lord blesses his people with peace." Psalm 29:11

"You will keep in perfect peace those whose minds are steadfast, because they trust in you." Isaiah 26:3

"Cast all your anxiety on him because he cares for you." 1 Peter 5:7

"I have said these things to you, that in me you may have peace. In the world you will have tribulation. But take heart; I have overcome the world." John 16:33

"Be careful for nothing; but in everything by prayer and supplication with thanksgiving let your requests be made known unto God. And the peace of God, which passeth all understanding, shall keep your hearts and minds through Christ Jesus." Philippians 4:6-7

"And let the peace of God rule in your hearts, to the which also ye are called in one body; and be ye thankful." Colossians 3:15

"Peace I leave with you, my peace I give unto you: not as the world giveth, give I unto you. Let not your heart be troubled, neither let it be afraid." John 14:27

"Depart from evil, and do good; seek peace, and pursue it." Psalms 34:14

"Now the God of hope fill you with all joy and peace in believing, that ye may abound in hope, through the power of the Holy Ghost." Romans 15:13

Conclusion

Be Gentle
With
Yourself

I'm glad that you've come this far. Toxicity comes with different faces and in different garbs. The moment you realize you're beginning to lose your sense of individuality, there's a problem. The moment you begin to seek wholeness and validation in another, you're likely to become toxic yourself. Why? You might end up manipulating another person into doing certain things just for you to feel good about yourself.

Toxicity is deeply rooted in our formative years or in past traumas—but we might not know what the other person is going through; we just feel this person is being a jerk. While we may make excuses for them depending on our relationship to them, we need to look out for ourselves. We should be careful not to form an identity out of a relationship. What if you're falling prey to someone's manipulation because you've failed to identify your own traumas? Note that traumas aren't only about what happened to you; they're also about what didn't. The first step to healing is identifying the fact that you might be an enabler of your abuse without even knowing it. Like the codependent, you're constantly pouring all of yourself into someone just to fill a void. The other person then begins to capitalize on your low self-worth to dominate you.

The world would be a better place if folks were committed to setting boundaries and sticking to them. If you have boundaries and are assertive about them, you won't easily become a doormat for others. Know when to say no—and when you do, mean it.

Self-awareness is a form of self-care, which will help you navigate a toxic relationship. This is how you achieve wholeness emotionally and psychologically. This is how you know when and how to set boundaries.

Practice the self-care techniques that have been mentioned in this book. If you need to, you can refer back to this book for reminders. Keep your head high.

Let the peace of the Lord keep and strengthen you, my dear reader.

Thank You

Thank you so much for purchasing my book.

You could have picked from so many other books, but you took a chance and chose this one.

So, THANK YOU SO MUCH for getting this book and for making it all the way to the end.

Before you go, I wanted to ask you for one small favor. **Could you please consider writing a review on Amazon? Posting a review is the best and easiest way to help other people gain true freedom by setting boundaries.**

Let's do this together! Your review will help other people discover the information in this book. Your review is very valuable, it will help me to keep writing the kinds of books that will help you get the results you want. I would love to hear from you.

>> Leave a review on Amazon US <<
Scan the QR code with your phone

>> Leave a review on Amazon UK <<
Scan the QR code with your phone

References

American Psychological Association. (n.d.). APA Dictionary of Psychology. *American Psychological Association*. Retrieved from https://dictionary.apa.org

American Psychiatric Association. (2013). Personality disorders. In *Diagnostic and Statistical Manual of Mental Disorders* (5th ed.). Washington, DC: American Psychiatric Publishing Inc.

Bame, Y. (2017). 3 in 4 US adults don't know what gaslighting is. *YouGov America*. Retrieved from https://today.yougov.com/topics/health/articles-reports/2017/06/27/it-could-be-happening-you-3-4-us-adults-dont-know-

Biggers, L. (2022). 9 signs of narcissistic personality disorder. *Duke Health*. Retrieved from https://www.dukehealth.org/blog/9-signs-of-narcissistic-personality-disorder

Bradberry, T. (2015). 10 toxic people you should avoid at all costs. *Forbes*. Retrieved from https://www.forbes.com/sites/travisbradberry/2015/11/10/10-toxic-people-you-should-avoid-at-all-costs/

Casabianca, S. (2021). Why do narcissists play the victim? *Psych Central.* Retrieved from https://psychcentral.com/disorders/narcissistic-personality-disorder/narcissist-plays-the-victim

Cikanavicius, D. (2019). Triangulation: The narcissist's best play. *Psych Central.* Retrieved from https://psychcentral.com/blog/psychology-self/2019/10/triangulation-and-narcissism

Cleveland Clinic (2020). Narcissistic personality disorder: Traits, tests, treatment. *Cleveland Clinic.* Retrieved from https://my.clevelandclinic.org/health/diseases/9742-narcissistic-personality-disorder

Ettensohn, M., & Simon, J. (2017). *Unmasking narcissism: A guide to understanding the narcissist in your life.* San Antonio, Texas: Althea Press.

Faith, C. (2009). Dependent personality disorder: A review of etiology and treatment. *Graduate Journal of Counseling Psychology, 1*(2). Retrieved from http://epublications.marquette.edu/gjcp/vol1/iss2/7?utm_source=epublications.marquette.edu%2Fgjcp%2Fvol1%2Fiss2%2F7&utm_medium=PDF&utm_campaign=PDFCoverPages

Guest User. (2019). The benefits of early childhood friendships and 3 tips for helping your child establish meaningful friendships. *Exchange Family Center*. Retrieved from https://www.exchangefamilycenter.org/exchange-family-center-blog/2019/10/1/the-benefits-of-early-childhood-friendships-and-3-tips-for-helping-your-child-establish-meaningful-friendships

Hasson, G. (2015). *How to deal with difficult people: Smart tactics for overcoming the problem people in your life* (2nd ed., Vol. 2). Mankato, Minnesota: Capstone.

Holzman, P. S. (2023). Personality. *Encyclopedia Britannica*. Retrieved from https://www.britannica.com/topic/personality

Jordan, K. (2021). Breaking up with a narcissist: 5 tips and what to expect. *Choosing Therapy*. Retrieved from https://www.choosingtherapy.com/breaking-up-with-a-narcissist/

Kacel, E. L., Ennis, N., & Pereira, D. B. (2017). Narcissistic personality disorder in clinical health psychology practice: Case studies of comorbid psychological distress and life-limiting illness. *Behavioral Medicine*, *43*(3), 156. doi:10.1080/08964289.2017.1301875

Lamothe, C. (2019). Love bombing: 10 signs to know. *Healthline*. Retrieved from https://www.healthline.com/health/love-bombing

Mancao, A. L. (2020). Not every narcissist has narcissistic personality disorder. *Mindbodygreen*. Retrieved from https://www.mindbodygreen.com/articles/not-every-narcissist-has-narcissistic-personality-disorder

Maritzer, T. (2021). How to communicate your needs in a relationship. *Marriage.com.* Retrieved from https://www.marriage.com/advice/communication/how-to-communicate-your-needs-in-a-relationship

Menczer, F., & Hills, T. (2020). Information overload helps fake news spread, and social media knows it. *Scientific American.* Retrieved from https://www.scientificamerican.com/article/information-overload-helps-fake-news-spread-and-social-media-knows-it/

Pies, R. (2011). How to eliminate narcissism overnight. Innovations in Clinical Neuroscience, *8*(2), 23–27. Retrieved from http://www.ncbi.nlm.nih.gov/pmc/articles/PMC3071092/

Ramsay, G., & Jolayemi, A. (2020). Personality disorders revisited: A newly proposed mental illness. *Cureus, 12*(8). doi:10.7759/cureus.9634

Roark, S. V. (2012). Narcissistic personality disorder: Effect on relationships. Retrieved from https://pubmed.ncbi.nlm.nih.gov/23472440/

Ronningstam, E., & Weinberg, I. (2013). Narcissistic personality disorder: Progress in recognition and treatment. *The Journal of Lifelong Learning in Psychiatry, XI*(2), 167–177. Retrieved from http://focus.psychiatryonline.org/data/Journals/FOCUS/9 26935/167.pdf

Sweet, P. L. (2022). How gaslighting manipulates reality. *Scientific American.* Retrieved from https://www.scientificamerican.com/article/how-gaslighting-manipulates-reality/

Telloian, C. (2021). How to break up with someone who has a narcissistic personality. Psych Central. Retrieved from https://psychcentral.com/health/breaking-up-with-a-narcissistic-personality

Tzu, S. (2006). *The art of war* (L. Giles, trans.). Filiquarian Publishing LLC.

Van der Kolk, B. (2014). *The body keeps the score: Brain, mind, and body in the healing of trauma.* New York: Viking Press.

Walton, J. (1996). Spiritual relationships. *Journal of Holistic Nursing, 14*(3), 237–250. doi:10.1177/089801019601400306

Other Sources

https://abusewarrior.com/abuse/manipulation-tactics/

https://psychcentral.com/blog/psychology-self/2019/10/triangulation-and-narcissism#1

https://www.youthkiawaaz.com/2022/05/the-end-was-necessary-a-toxic-relationship/

https://www.mindtools.com/aorqe4z/building-good-work-relationships

https://everydaypower.com/toxic-relationships-quotes/

https://www.womansday.com/life/a40059190/narcissist-quotes/

https://fortuneandframe.com/blogs/news/self-care-quotes

https://lanredahunsi.com/top-quotes-on-codependency/

https://www.happierhuman.com/toxic-relationship-quotes/